English for
Banking & Finance

2

Course Book

Marjorie Rosenberg

Series editor David Bonamy

Contents

Money matters

- understand and use basic financial terms
- explain personal banking habits and facts
- describe different types of financial organisations
- understand and explain how investment banks work

Managing your finances

Reading   **1**   Look at Maria's bank statement. Complete her account summary.

First Bank

Ms Maria Roberts
68 Glenridge Road
Birmingham
BR5 5QT
United Kingdom

23 December to 22 January
Account name: Ms Maria Roberts

Account summary

Opening balance	£2,300
Payments in	£(1) _____
Payments out	£(2) _____
Closing balance	£3,714
Overdraft limit	£2,100
IBAN:	GB10FIRST43760959233021
BIC:	FIRSTGB6043C
Sort code:	437609
Account number:	59233021
Sheet number:	20

A Your current account details

Date	Payment type	Details	Paid out	Paid in	Balance
22 Dec		**Balance brought forward**			**£2,300**
23 Dec	Transfer	**B** Salary		£2,423	£4,723
27 Dec	Withdrawal	**C** ATM No. 32	£250		£4,473
31 Dec	Credit	**D** Interest		£34	£4,507
04 Jan	**E** Standing order	Rent	£450		£4,057
06 Jan	**F** Direct debit	Telephone	£57		£4,000
15 Jan	Direct debit	Home insurance	£68		£3,932
21 Jan	Direct debit	Credit card	£218		£3,714
			£1,043	**£2,457**	
		G Balance carried forward			£3,714

IBAN =
International Bank
Account Number
BIC = Bank
Identifier Code
ATM = Automated
Teller Machine

2   Match sentences 1–7 to letters A–G on the bank statement in 1.

1   Maria has a current account. ____
2   Maria sees how much money she has at the end of the month. ____
3   She pays her rent every month by standing order. ____
4   She pays other bills by direct debit. ____
5   She withdraws cash at ATMs. ____
6   She receives her salary on the 23rd of the month. ____
7   She receives interest once a year. ____

Vocabulary   **3**   Complete these sentences with the words in the box.

ATM	balance	credit	current account	direct debit
home insurance	rent	salary	standing order	withdrawal

1   My _____ shows how much money I have in my account.
2   I have a(n) _____ at my bank to make payments and receive money.
3   I see a(n) _____ on my account when someone pays money into it.
4   I usually get cash out of my account at a(n) _____ .
5   I make the same payment every month with a(n) _____ .
6   My employer pays my _____ into my account.
7   I have _____ to protect my home.
8   I pay bills each month automatically. I use _____ .
9   Every month I pay _____ for my flat.
10 I take money from my account. It is a(n) _____ .

Speaking   **4**   Work in pairs. Look at Peter's monthly budget and answer these questions.

1   How much does Peter pay for insurance every month?
2   How much salary does Peter receive?
3   How much does Peter pay for petrol every month?

Income		Outgoings	
salary	£1,821	rent	£575
		food	£370
		electricity: monthly payment	£56
		home insurance: monthly payment	£28
		credit card	£126
		pension contributions	£115
		clothes	£24
		car insurance: monthly payment	£42
		petrol	£35
		savings	£150
		other	£220

Language

Present simple

We use the **present simple** to talk about facts, repeated actions and habits.	My current account **doesn't pay** interest. (fact) She **pays** her rent every month by standing order. (repeated action) We **withdraw** cash at an ATM. (habit)

5   Look at the questions in 4. Write five more questions about Peter's income and outgoings. Then ask a partner.

A: How much does Peter pay for rent every month?
B: He pays £575.

Speaking   **6**   Write your own monthly budget. Show your income and outgoings. What is your balance at the end of the month? Ask your partner about their monthly budget. Do they have any direct debits or standing orders? Which bills do they pay with them?

Writing   **7**   Write a short report about the money that you spend each month.

Every month I receive ... . I pay for ... . I buy ... .

Finance and the economy

Speaking **1** Work in pairs. What activities do these illustrations represent? Are these activities important for the economy? Why/Why not? Use the words in the box to help you.

buy	factory	finance	housing market	manufacturing
produce	retailing	sell		

Vocabulary **2** Match words 1–9 to definitions a–i.

1	loss	a)	money that you borrow from a bank	
2	demand	b)	selling something for less than you buy it for	
3	share	c)	money that you pay to borrow money	
4	interest	d)	ownership of part of a company	
5	investment	e)	income greater than expenses	
6	supply	f)	goods and services that people sell	
7	profit	g)	money that you borrow to buy a house or flat	
8	loan	h)	money that is put into a business	
9	mortgage	i)	goods and services that people want to buy	

Reading **3** Complete this introduction to finance from a consumer website with words from 2.

The economy and the world of finance

Two key principles of the economy are supply and demand. Some people have goods or services to sell and other people want to buy those goods or services. The relationship between supply and (1) _____ is very important. The world of finance is a necessary part of the economy.

People need money to do business. Banks first collect money from customers. Then they lend money to people or institutions. Customers who borrow money pay (2) _____ to the bank until they pay the money back. There are different types of (3) _____ . For example, people who want to buy a house or flat usually choose a(n) (4) _____ .

(5) _____ in shares of stock is another part of the financial world. People buy shares and then own a part of a company. They hope to make a(n) (6) _____ when the company does well. When the company does not do well, the investor makes a(n) (7) _____ .

These are some of the ways that financial institutions help the economy.

4 Match 1–6 to a–f to make sentences.

1 Customers pay interest on	a) money to customers.
2 The economy needs	b) make investments?
3 Banks often lend	c) lend money to every customer.
4 Do you sometimes	d) a mortgage?
5 We don't	e) money they borrow.
6 Do they have	f) strong financial institutions.

5 Which sentences in 4 are facts? Mark these *F*. Which are repeated actions or habits? Mark these *R/H*.

Speaking **6** Work in pairs. Discuss these questions.

1 Why is the relationship between supply and demand important?
2 In your country, which goods and services are popular?
3 Do the prices of these goods and services change often? Give examples.

Vocabulary **7** Match words 1–4 to their opposites a–d.

1 borrow	a) sell
2 loss	b) supply
3 demand	c) lend
4 buy	d) profit

8 Write sentences with the words in 7.

There is a big supply of houses but there is no demand for them.

Listening **9** ▶ 🔊 **02** Listen to two telephone conversations and match speakers 1 and 2 to sentences a–c. There is one extra sentence.

a) This customer has a question about interest. ___
b) This customer wants to invest in a company. ___
c) This customer needs a mortgage. ___

10 Now complete the conversations with words from 7. Then listen again and check your answers.

1 A: Good morning. AFC Bank, can I help you?
   B: Good morning. I am a customer of the bank and I want to (1) _____ some money.
   A: Yes, sir. Which department do you want? Er … what is the money for?
   B: I want to (2) _____ a flat.
   A: Just a moment. Oh yes, Mr Sharma is free.

2 A: Good morning, I am interested in shares of NewCom.
   B: Oh yes. Just a moment. I see that the price is quite high at the moment.
   A: I don't want to buy expensive shares and sell them for less. I don't want to make a(n) (3) _____ .
   B: I understand. AllTech looks good today. The (4) _____ for their shares is not so high at the moment.
   A: That sounds interesting. I want to make a(n) (5) _____ with this investment.

Speaking **11** Work in pairs. Discuss these questions. Give details.

1 Do you pay rent or do you own a flat?
2 Do you have a mortgage? Do you pay interest on it?
3 Do you get interest on your current account?
4 Do you make investments?

Banks and building societies

Vocabulary **1** Match words 1–6 to definitions a–f.

1 merger a) you use money in this account every day
2 takeover bid b) two companies become one company
3 pension c) you save money in this account over a long time
4 current account d) one company tries to buy another company
5 deposit account e) a special bank for deposit accounts and mortgages
6 building society f) you save this money for when you stop working

Listening **2** ▶ **03** Listen to three conversations and match speakers 1–3 to the financial institutions they work in A–C.

A retail bank

B building society

C investment bank

3 Work in pairs. Look at activities 1–9 below. Discuss which activities the institutions in 2 do. You can match some activities to more than one type of financial institution.

1 arrange mergers ___
2 help customers save for pensions ___
3 arrange takeover bids ___
4 offer current accounts ___
5 mostly arrange mortgages ___
6 give financial advice to companies ___
7 take deposits from customers ___
8 help companies sell their shares ___
9 offer special deposit accounts ___

4 ▶ **04** Listen to three experts and check your answers in 3.

Speaking **5** List some examples of the institutions in 2. Then work in pairs and compare your lists. Do any names appear on both lists?

Language

Present simple with adverbs of frequency and time expressions

We use the **present simple** with adverbs of frequency and time expressions to say how often something happens.	*I **often give** financial advice to companies.*
Adverbs of frequency (e.g. *usually, mostly, often, sometimes, seldom, rarely, never*) come after the verb *be* and before other verbs.	*I **am rarely** late to work.* *He **never arranges** takeover bids.*
Time expressions (e.g. *every day/week/month, in the morning/ afternoon/evening, on Monday, from Monday to Friday*) come at the beginning or end of the sentence.	*We advise customers **from Monday to Friday**.* *I open accounts for customers **every day**.*

6 Write five sentences about one of the institutions in 2. Then read them to a partner and ask him/her to guess the institution.

They usually/mostly/never ...

Vocabulary **7** What are these people doing? Match sentences 1–8 to illustrations A–H.

A Do you want to deposit this in your current account?

B How do I pay the money back?

C How much does the flat cost?

D

E

F What kind of account do you need?

G What kind of insurance do you need?

H How much interest does the deposit account pay?

1 They are talking about a mortgage. ___
2 He is opening his safety deposit box. ___
3 They are talking about interest on savings. ___
4 She is withdrawing money from her account. ___
5 They are discussing insurance. ___
6 She is depositing money into her account. ___
7 They are talking about the terms of a loan. ___
8 He is opening an account. ___

Language

Present continuous

We use the **present continuous** to talk about actions happening now, at the moment of speaking. We often use it with time words such as *now*, *right now*, *currently* or *at the moment*.	He**'s opening** a current account at the moment. **Is** he **withdrawing** money from his account? Yes, he **is**./No, he **isn't**.
We don't use stative verbs (e.g. *like*, *know*, *want*) in the present continuous.	I **don't need** a current account at the moment.

8 Read this part of an advertisement for Heart of Gold Building Society. Complete it with the correct present simple or present continuous form of the verbs in brackets.

This is why we always (1) _____ (offer) the best interest rates to our customers. We (2) _____ (want) to give *you* the profits. At the moment we (3) _____ (offer) special current accounts and deposit accounts to new customers. We also (4) _____ (know) that many customers (5) _____ (want) to buy a house or flat. That is why we (6) _____ (feel) that loans for housing (7) _____ (be) important. We (8) _____ (arrange) special terms now for first-time customers. We (9) _____ (believe) our products are just what you need. So what (10) _____ (you / wait) for? We (11) _____ (be) here to help you. Our doors (12) _____ (be) open from 8 to 5 Monday to Friday.

Writing **9** Write a short paragraph describing what an institution you use offers and what is happening there at the moment.

My local building society offers very good mortgage deals. At the moment they are charging four percent interest.

Investment banks

Vocabulary

1 What do investment banks do? Match phrases 1–5 to definitions a–e.

1 issue shares

2 fight takeover bids

3 raise capital
4 underwrite securities
5 give financial advice

a) work against someone trying to buy a company
b) help someone with money and investments
c) offer parts of a company to investors
d) get money to run a business
e) arrange to sell shares to investors and to guarantee a minimum price

2 Complete these sentences with the words in the box.

> acquisition   analyst   Brokerage Department   buyout   investment fund
> IPO   merger   stock market   strategic planning

1 A(n) _____ stands for 'initial public offering'. It is the first time a company sells its shares to investors.
2 A company does _____ so it is ready for the future.
3 The _____ is the section of a bank which buys and sells shares for customers.
4 A(n) _____ happens when a company or person buys another business. This is also called a(n) _____ .
5 A(n) _____ is a fund which takes money from all its clients and invests it.
6 A(n) _____ looks at information and decides what to do with it.
7 When two companies join together to make one, this is a(n) _____ .
8 People buy shares on the _____ .

Language

Definite article (*the*), indefinite article (*a, an*) and zero article	
We use **the** before groups and nationalities or when there is only one of something.	**The** British don't generally use pre-paid credit cards.
We use **a(n)** before a job or place of work, and to talk about something or someone that is part of a group.	I'm **a** mortgage adviser. What do you do?
We use **no article** before company names, days, months and years, and before plural nouns, to talk about something in general.	Shoba has an interview at HSBC on Wednesday.

3 Complete these sentences with *a, an, the* or no article (–).

1 Do you have _____ current account?
2 What _____ accounts does your bank offer?
3 Is there _____ ATM in your bank?
4 Do you know what _____ interest rate is this week on loans?
5 Is there _____ investment bank in your town/city?
6 Why does a customer need _____ standing order?

Speaking

4 Work in pairs. Discuss the questions in 3.

Review

1 ▶ 🎧 05 Listen and match speakers 1–7 to activities a–h. There is one extra activity.

    a) opening a deposit account ___
    b) getting a safety deposit box ___
    c) arranging a buyout ___
    d) fighting a takeover bid ___
    e) asking about a mortgage ___
    f) asking about strategic planning ___
    g) asking about a current account ___
    h) thinking about an IPO ___

2 Complete these sentences with the correct present simple or present continuous form of the verbs in brackets.

    1 In my job I _____ (give) advice to clients about mortgages.
    2 Building societies _____ (usually / not offer) current accounts.
    3 Today I _____ (give) financial advice to a new client.
    4 Mr and Mrs Smith _____ (want) to buy a flat this year.
    5 What _____ (you / like) about your job at the bank?
    6 Our bank _____ (be) open from 8 to 5.
    7 This week we _____ (issue) shares for a client and we _____ (sell) them on the stock market.
    8 He _____ (usually / help) customers with mortgages.

3 Complete these sentences with *a, an, the* or no article (–).

    1 He is _____ analyst at _____ investment bank in London.
    2 She works in _____ Brokerage Department at _____ Atlantic Bank.
    3 They are _____ investment bankers.
    4 We work at _____ building society in Vienna.
    5 _____ job I have in Dubai is great.

4 Match 1–6 to a–f to make sentences.

    1 Retail banks always
    2 In some countries banks never
    3 Investment banks usually
    4 Companies sometimes
    5 Customers often
    6 Building societies mostly

    a) withdraw money from the ATM.
    b) give advice to companies.
    c) offer cheques to customers.
    d) offer current accounts.
    e) offer mortgages.
    f) make takeover bids.

5 Work in pairs. Student A, look at the information on this page. Student B, look at the information on page 70. Follow the instructions.

Student A
You are a customer. You hear that the building societies Homemaker and Save and Build are merging. Ask Student B, a Homemaker employee, for details.

6 Work in pairs. Answer this question using adverbs of frequency and time expressions.

What sort of things do you do in your job?
In my job I always/never/mostly ...

Products in retail banking

- find out what a customer needs a
  give advice
- give and check instructions
- talk about the future
- express present and future abilit
- compare details of products

Bank products

Listening 1 A bank clerk is helping a new customer to open an account. Work in pairs. Which of these phrases do you expect to hear in the conversation?

1 ☐ use the cash dispenser
2 ☐ deposit money
3 ☐ receive your salary by direct deposit
4 ☐ make withdrawals
5 ☐ pay bills
6 ☐ arrange direct debits
7 ☐ set up standing orders
8 ☐ get a bank card
9 ☐ open a current account
10 ☐ get a statement of account

2 ▶ 🔊 06 Read the phrases in 1 again. Listen to the conversation and tick ✓ the phrases you hear.

3 Listen again and answer these questions.

1 Why does the customer need an account?
2 How can she receive her salary?
3 How can she pay her bills?
4 Where can she make withdrawals?
5 Does she decide to open an account?

Vocabulary 4 Match words and phrases 1–5 to definitions a–e.

1 direct deposit
2 statement of account

3 amount

4 bank card
5 deposit

a) quantity
b) a document that shows the activity in your account
c) a card you use to withdraw cash at the cash dispenser
d) money put into an account
e) a way to receive your salary directly

cash dispenser = ATM

Language

Modals for ability and possibility: *can*	
We use **can** + infinitive to talk about possibility or ability in the present.	**Can** you help me? I **can't** right now. **Can** you wait a minute? No, I'm afraid I **can't**.

5 Work in pairs. Ask and answer questions about this product using *can* or *can't*.

A: Can I get monthly statements online with this account?
B: Yes, you can.

Features of the Special Saver account:

get monthly statement online	✓	make withdrawals at any time	✓
use cash dispenser 24/7	✓	set up standing orders	✓
make deposits on Sundays	✗	set up direct debits	✓
receive salary by direct deposit	✓	get monthly statements by post	✗

Reading **6** Read the customer information from the website of a bank. Are these sentences *true* (T), *false* (F) or is there *no information* in the text (NI)?

1 The bank offers current and deposit accounts, and loans. ___
2 You can get a safe deposit box. ___
3 You can earn interest with a current account. ___
4 You can talk to an expert about your financial needs. ___
5 Customers can only use cash dispensers at the bank. ___
6 You receive statements by post once a month. ___
7 You can only get short-term loans at this bank. ___
8 You need a bank card to withdraw money from the cash dispenser. ___

Universal Bank

We are a full service bank and offer products to both large and small customers. For people who want to regularly deposit and withdraw money, we suggest opening a current account with us. You can receive your salary through direct deposit and pay your bills through direct debit. With your bank card you can withdraw money from cash dispensers everywhere and at any time. You can also get your statements of account from the machines at the bank so you know how much money you have in your account.

For people who want to save money, we suggest a deposit account. With this account you can save money for the future and earn interest on it. We have both long-term and short-term deposit accounts. You can decide.

And when you need to borrow money, you can come to us. We arrange long-term or short-term loans. Whatever your financial needs are, we are here to help. Talk to one of our experts today!

Language

Making suggestions and recommendations	
Finding out what a customer needs	*Can I help you?* *Do you need to withdraw money?* *Would you like to see your account online?*
Giving a customer advice	*I suggest/recommend a deposit account.* *I suggest/recommend opening a current account.* *Then you need a standing order.*

7 Work in pairs. Take turns to ask a customer questions and make suggestions based on the customer information in 6.

Do you need to deposit money regularly into your account?
Then I suggest a current account.

Speaking **8** Work in pairs. Student A, look at the information on page 68. Student B, look at the information on page 70. Follow the instructions.

Online banking

Vocabulary **1** Look at Sven Johnson's online banking account. What can he do online? Match 1–6 to A–F.

1 change an amount ___
2 check how much money he has ___
3 look at amounts received ___

4 make a payment ___
5 move funds from one account to another ___
6 print out the page ___

⊖ ⊖ ⊖
◄ ► | c | + | |
m |

A 🖶   Sven Johnson

● account details   ● sort code   **C** ● payments to account
● account number   **B** ● balance   ● payments from account

● current accounts   **D** ● update standing orders   **F** ● transfer money
● deposit accounts   ● update direct debits   ● change a payment
● view statement   **E** ● pay a bill   ● personal loans

---

2 Look at this online banking web page. Then complete the sentences below with words from the web page.

m   »

Become an online banking customer today! Discover how easy online banking is!
With online banking you will be able to:

★ view your transactions.
★ keep track of your money.
★ download and print your statements.
★ check your real-time balance.

★ make payments.
★ manage standing orders and direct debits.
★ transfer money.
★ choose your own password.

1 The amount of money in your account is your _____ .
2 When you regularly check how much money is in your account, you _____ of your money.
3 When you move money from one account to another, you _____ it.
4 With online banking you can _____ the transactions you make straight away.
5 You can _____ your regular payments like direct debits and standing orders.
6 You can _____ your statements of account to your computer.
7 When you have bills to pay, you can make _____ online.

Language

Future possibility and ability with *will* and *be able to*

We use *will* + *be able to* + infinitive to say that something will be possible or someone will have the ability to do something in the future.	You *will be able to transfer* money from one account to another.
We use *will* + **subject** + *be able to* + infinitive for questions, and *will not* or *won't* + *be able to* + infinitive for negative sentences.	*Will* he *be able to download* his statements? Yes, he *will.*/No, he *won't.*
After *will*, we use *be able to* (not *can/can't*).	You *won't be able to view* another person's accounts.

Speaking 3 Work in pairs. Take turns being the customer and the bank employee. Ask and answer three questions about what you will be able to do with an online banking account.

A: *Will I be able to borrow money?*
B: *No, you won't.*
A: *Will I be able to see my statements?*
B: *Yes, you will.*

Reading 4 Work in pairs. Put the words in the box together and complete these online banking tips.

| act | ance | bal | but | fer | ion | ment | pass | state | ton | trans | word |

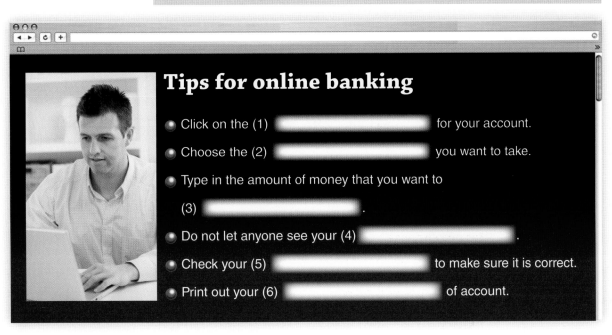

Tips for online banking

- Click on the (1) _____ for your account.
- Choose the (2) _____ you want to take.
- Type in the amount of money that you want to

  (3) _____ .
- Do not let anyone see your (4) _____ .
- Check your (5) _____ to make sure it is correct.
- Print out your (6) _____ of account.

Language

The imperative

Imperative verbs do not have a subject. The sentence begins with a verb.	***Click*** on the button. ***Don't let*** anyone see your password.

Writing 5 Write three more online banking tips. Begin each one with an imperative verb.

Speaking 6 Work in pairs. Take turns to give each other advice on using the online banking web page in 1 on page 14.

A: *I want to change a monthly payment.*
B: *Click on 'update standing orders' and change the amount.*

1 I need to pay my tax.
2 I want to check how much money I have.
3 I want to take money from my current account and put it in my savings account.
4 I need a copy of my statement on my computer.
5 I need a paper copy of my statement.
6 I give money to charity every month. I want to give more.

Telephone helplines

Listening **1** ▶ 🎧 07 Listen to a conversation between an online banking customer and a customer adviser and answer these questions.

1 What problem does Mr Chatterjee have?
2 What does he need to provide to the bank representative?
3 How can he see the page for his account?
4 On the 'Proceed' page, what does the information on the right ask?
5 How can he see his statement?
6 What does Mr Chatterjee do at the end?
7 What does the bank representative tell Mr Chatterjee to do the next time he has a problem?

Language

Sequencers	
Use *first*, *next*, *now*, *then*, *after that*, *at the end* or *finally* to indicate a sequence of actions or instructions.	*First* log in to your account. *Next* click on the action. *Now* type in an amount. *Then* press 'Enter'. *After that* you can see your new balance. *Finally* you can log out.

Writing **2** You are training a customer adviser for the helpline. Write these notes in the correct order for a new employee. Use sequencing words and the imperative.

First say the name … . Then …

★ What does the customer need?
★ Goodbye.
★ This is what you do.
★ customer's name and account number
★ Is everything clear?
★ name of bank

Speaking **3** Work in pairs. Student A, look at the information on this page. Student B, look at the information on page 70. Follow the instructions.

Student A

1 You are an online banking helpdesk representative. Explain to a customer how to transfer money from an online account using the information below.
2 Swap roles. Listen to Student B and take notes.

1 log in – password	**4** type in amount
2 choose action – 'Transfer'	**5** click 'Enter'
3 type in name, account number	**6** log out

Reading 4 Read this leaflet. Who is the course for?

   a) managers
   b) customer advisers
   c) all bank employees

In-company telephone training ☎

Learn how to help customers on the phone.
On this two-day course you will:

- practise finding out what customers need.
- find out how to give them information they want.
- learn how to give good customer service.

At the end of the course you will be able to help customers with all their needs. The course will take place on Tuesday and Wednesday, from 9 a.m. to 5 p.m.

Language

Future forms

We use **will** to make predictions and talk about decisions made at the time of speaking and timetabled events.	*The course **will take** place on Tuesday.* *We **won't be** in the office on Wednesday.*
We use the **present continuous** and **be going to** + infinitive to talk about plans or intentions.	*Our team **is travelling** to the conference tomorrow morning.* *You **are going to practise** finding out what customers need.*

5 Jan has decided to take the telephone training course. Complete her email using *will*, *be going to* or the present continuous.

Hi Latifa,

Our company (1) _____ (offer) a telephone training course next week and I (2) _____ (take) part in it. I think it (3) _____ (be) very interesting. I hope I (4) _____ (learn) more about customer service in this course. It is not always easy to talk to customers on the phone. But I think at the end I (5) _____ (be) able to help customers with different problems. We (6) _____ (have) the training here at the company, so I (7) _____ (not be) at my desk on Tuesday. I (8) _____ (tell) you all about it at lunch on Wednesday. See you then.

Best,
Jan

Speaking 6 Work in pairs. You are going on a telephone training course. Look at the email in 5 and answer these questions.

   1 When will the course take place?
   2 What are you going to learn?
   3 At the end of the course, what will you be able to do?

7 Work in pairs. Imagine your company is going to offer a course in telephone skills. What would you like to learn? Discuss.

Comparing products

1 Read this extract from the UBE Bank website and match words and phrases 1–7 to definitions a–g.

Banks offer (1) <u>convenient</u> (2) <u>access to funds</u> as well as facilities like overdrafts and (3) <u>long-term</u> loans. An (4) <u>overdraft</u> is usually more (5) <u>expensive</u> than a loan but easier to arrange. At UBE we believe we offer the most competitive products and the best service. Please click here to see our list of (6) <u>fees and charges</u>, and the current (7) <u>interest rates</u> for savings and loans.

a) the ability to use your money ___
b) easy ___
c) prices of bank services ___
d) lasting for a long period of time ___
e) costing a lot of money ___
f) rates for borrowing or saving ___
g) a negative balance on the account ___

Language

Comparative and superlative adjectives

	Adjective	Comparative	Superlative
One- and most two-syllable adjectives	*easy*	*easier **(than)***	*the **easiest***
Two or more syllable adjectives	*expensive*	***more/less** expensive **(than)***	***the most/least** expensive*
Irregular adjectives	*good* *bad*	*better **(than)*** *worse **(than)***	***the** best* ***the** worst*
All adjectives	*high*	***(not) as** high **as***	

2 Complete these sentences with the comparative or superlative form of the adjectives in brackets.

1 An overdraft is _____ (expensive) way to borrow money.
2 Online banking is _____ (easy) going to the bank.
3 This is _____ (high) rate you can get.
4 An ATM is _____ (convenient) waiting at the bank.
5 The fees and charges for a mortgage at the building society are _____ (low) the ones at the bank.

Speaking **3** Work in pairs. Compare the products in the box. Use the language in the Language box and the words in this table.

current account   deposit account   mortgage
online banking   overdraft facility   short-term loan

Adjectives	Other words
convenient expensive easy-to-use complicated common necessary	manage money access to funds interest rate password keep track of set up

An overdraft is more convenient than a short-term loan but it is more expensive.

Review

Language **1** Look at these minutes from a meeting and write a memo giving instructions to customer advisers. Use the imperative.

> **1** It is a bad idea to give your employee password to anyone else.
>
> **2** It is a good idea to keep your company ID card in a safe place.
>
> **3** It is a good idea to be polite to customers.
>
> **4** It is a bad idea to forget a customer's name.

2 Match 1–5 to a–e to make instructions on how to use online banking. Then put the instructions in the correct order.

1 ☐ After that you can transfer money
2 ☐ Then look at the
3 ☐7 First log in
4 ☐ Finally remember to
5 ☐ Next click

a) different actions you can choose from.
b) log out.
c) on the one you want.
d) with your password.
e) or change standing orders, for example.

3 Complete this email using *will* or *be going to*.

I have big plans for next week. It (1) _____ (be) very exciting because I (2) _____ (learn) to use English for our telephone helpline. I hope I (3) _____ (not have) any problems understanding the people who call. My hours (4) _____ (be) from 8 to 5. I think I (5) _____ (answer) questions about cash dispensers, online banking and our banking hours. I hope I (6) _____ (not forget) anything important. My boss (7) _____ (help) me at the beginning. After that I hope I (8) _____ (be) able to do everything perfectly!

Writing **4** Complete this email to a client. Compare the following:
1 arranging an overdraft with arranging a loan
2 an overdraft facility with a long-term loan and a short-term loan
3 online banking with waiting at the bank
4 interest rates for deposit accounts with interest rates for current accounts

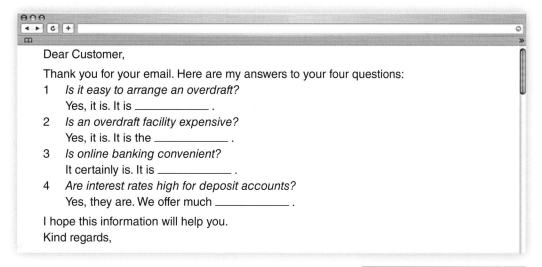

Dear Customer,

Thank you for your email. Here are my answers to your four questions:
1 *Is it easy to arrange an overdraft?*
    Yes, it is. It is _____ .
2 *Is an overdraft facility expensive?*
    Yes, it is. It is the _____ .
3 *Is online banking convenient?*
    It certainly is. It is _____ .
4 *Are interest rates high for deposit accounts?*
    Yes, they are. We offer much _____ .

I hope this information will help you.
Kind regards,

3 Personal loans and credit

- ask for and give information usin
  modals and conditional forms
- complete an application form
- offer options
- agree and disagree politely
- explain and answer questions abc
  the terms of loans and mortgages

Credit and debit cards

Speaking **1** Work in pairs. Look at the cards in the photo and discuss these questions.

APR = annual
percentage rate
(the rate of interest
per year)

1 What are these cards for?
2 Which one(s) do you have?
3 Does your bank issue them?
4 Do other institutions issue them?
5 Do you know how much the APR is on credit cards?
6 If you don't have a credit card, why not?

I have/don't have a(n) … because …
I use my card to …

Vocabulary **2** Work in pairs. Match definitions 1–9 to the words and phrases in the 'magic table'. Write a number in each box. When you finish, the columns and rows will all add up to 15.

1 what you pay to borrow money from a bank or other financial institution
2 give someone money for a fixed time
3 a decision about how safe it is to lend money to a person or company
4 the maximum amount of money that you can spend with a single credit card
5 how you have to pay money back to a bank
6 when you buy something now and pay for it later
7 when you do not pay an amount you borrowed right away but later
8 the lowest amount that you can repay when you buy things on credit
9 take money directly out of a bank account

☐ credit	☐ carry a balance	☐ lend money	= 15
☐ interest	☐ repayment terms	☐ debit	= 15
☐ minimum payment	☐ credit rating	☐ credit limit	= 15
= 15	= 15	= 15	

Reading **3** Work in pairs. Read this information from a bank's intranet. Take turns to choose a word or phrase from the text and explain it to your partner. Your partner guesses what it is.

A: the lowest amount customers can pay when they owe money on a credit card
B: minimum payment

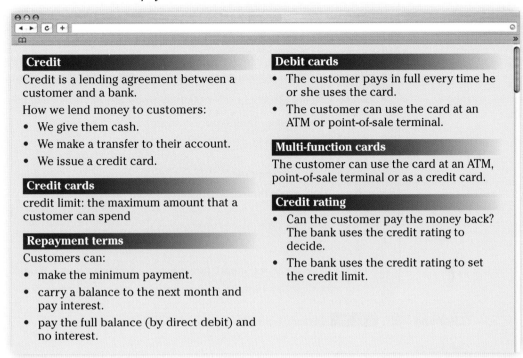

Credit
Credit is a lending agreement between a customer and a bank.
How we lend money to customers:
- We give them cash.
- We make a transfer to their account.
- We issue a credit card.

Credit cards
credit limit: the maximum amount that a customer can spend

Repayment terms
Customers can:
- make the minimum payment.
- carry a balance to the next month and pay interest.
- pay the full balance (by direct debit) and no interest.

Debit cards
- The customer pays in full every time he or she uses the card.
- The customer can use the card at an ATM or point-of-sale terminal.

Multi-function cards
The customer can use the card at an ATM, point-of-sale terminal or as a credit card.

Credit rating
- Can the customer pay the money back? The bank uses the credit rating to decide.
- The bank uses the credit rating to set the credit limit.

Language

Zero conditional	
We use the **zero conditional** to talk about general truths. We form zero conditional sentences with *if/when* + present simple + present simple.	*They only **pay** interest **if/when** they **carry** a balance.*
The *if* clause can come before or after the main clause in the sentence. When it comes at the beginning, we put a comma after it.	*If they **pay** the minimum balance, they **carry** the rest.* *We **don't charge** interest if they **pay** the whole amount.*

4 Match 1–5 to a–e to make zero conditional sentences.

1 If you pay your balance at the end of the month,
2 Do you use a credit card
3 If you use a debit card,
4 If a customer carries a balance over,
5 We charge interest if

a) we take the money from your account.
b) they pay interest on it.
c) a customer doesn't pay the whole amount at once.
d) when you go shopping?
e) we do not charge interest.

Speaking **5** Work in pairs. Discuss these questions.

1 What happens if you have a credit card and you only make the minimum payment every month?
2 What happens if you carry a balance on your credit card?
3 How much does the customer pay if they use a debit card?
4 What happens if a customer does not have a good credit rating?

Plastic money

Reading **1** Complete this leaflet about a new multi-function card with words from the magic table on page 20.

> Do you travel the world? Does shopping everywhere sound interesting to you? Then call us to find out about our new multi-function Champion (1) _____ Card!
>
> If you have a Champion card, you:
>
> - can pay for food, a hotel room, a concert ticket or rent a car without cash.
> - can choose the (2) _____ option and pay for purchases immediately.
> - can withdraw money from cash dispensers around the world.
> - can arrange a(n) (3) _____ with your bank.
> - can carry a(n) (4) _____ over from one month to the next.
> - will get a bill every month, which shows how much (5) _____ you have to pay.
> - can choose your (6) _____ and decide exactly how you want to pay back your credit.
>
> To find out more about this great offer, just ask your bank about our card.

Listening **2** ▶ 🎵 08 Listen to a radio spot and check your answers in 1.

Language

First conditional

We use the **first conditional** to talk about something that might happen in the future, as a result of a possible action or situation. We form first conditional sentences with *if* + present simple + *will/can/may* + infinitive.	*If you **have** a Champion card, you **will get** travel insurance.* *If you **have** a Champion card, you **can pay** for a hotel.*
The *if* clause can come before or after the main clause in the sentence. When it comes at the beginning, we put a comma after it.	*You **will not have** any problems with online shopping **if** you **have** a Champion card.* *If you **have** a Champion card, you **will not have** any problems with online shopping.*

3 Put these words in the correct order to make first conditional sentences. Start with the word in bold and add commas where necessary.

1 you / **if** / at the bank this afternoon / are / see / I / you / will
2 my credit card / **if** / lose / I / call / I / the bank / right away / will
3 a multi-function card / she / **if** / has / can / she / from an ATM / money / withdraw
4 easy to shop online / be / **it** / will / have / you / a credit card / if
5 get / **you** / can / travel insurance / a Champion card / if / have / you
6 a Champion card / may need / **he** / to use ATMs / around the world / he / wants / if

Speaking **4** Work in pairs. What can you do with the Champion card? Discuss. Use the first conditional.

If I have this card, I can/will ...
You may ... if ...

Listening 5 ▶ 🎵 09 Listen to two conversations and number these sentences and phrases in the order you hear them. Write a number in each box.

☐ That's not a bad idea. ___   ☐ I see your point. ___
☐ I couldn't agree more. ___   ☐ Yes, but ... ___
☐ It is out of the question ... ___

6 Do we use the sentences and phrases in 5 to *agree* (A) or *disagree* (D)? Write *A* or *D* on the lines in 5.

Speaking 7 Work in pairs. Look at the leaflet in 1 on page 22 again and discuss which three points are most important to you. Use phrases for agreeing and disagreeing.

Reading 8 Complete this FAQ web page with questions a–e.

FAQ = frequently asked questions

a) How can I add money to the card?   d) Why is it useful?
b) Who is it for?   e) What does it cost?
c) How can I get it?

The Champion Youth Pre-Paid Card

(1) ___
The benefits of the card:
• You do not need a bank account or credit rating.
• If you lose the card, you can <u>transfer</u> the amount left on it to a new card.
• You can use it at <u>point-of-sale</u> <u>terminals</u> all over the world.
• You can withdraw cash from <u>ATMs</u> everywhere.

(2) ___
This card is for you if:
• you do not have your own bank account.
• you want to <u>shop online</u>.
• you need a card for a <u>trip</u>.

(3) ___
The card is not expensive.
• The card costs €20 a year.
• A <u>replacement</u> card is <u>free</u>.
• You pay only €3.50 to withdraw cash.

(4) ___
It is easy to put money on the card.
• Do this directly at your bank from any of your accounts.
• Make transfers to the card online.
• Your parents can load money onto the card.

(5) ___
Come and talk to us at the bank.
• <u>Fill out</u> the form and <u>load</u> your new card with the amount you want.
• Go to our website, fill out the form and <u>order</u> the card online.

Vocabulary 9 Work in pairs. Look at the web page in 8 again and match these definitions with the underlined words.

1 journey _____
2 something that you don't pay for _____
3 something that takes the place of something else _____
4 move money from an account to another _____
5 cash dispenser _____

6 put money on a card _____
7 complete a form with information _____
8 a machine in a shop where you pay with a card and PIN code _____
9 request something _____
10 buy things over the internet _____

Speaking 10 Work in pairs or small groups. Look at the web page in 8 again and discuss these questions. Use conditional sentences where possible.

1 What happens if you lose the card?
2 How can you order the card online?
3 How can you put money on the card?
4 Where can you use the card?
5 What other benefits does this card have?

Personal loans and overdrafts

Vocabulary

1 Complete these sentences with the correct form of the words and phrases in the box. You do not need all the words/phrases.

> apply for/application form   authorised/authorisation   cash flow
> cover (overdraft/expenses)   instalment   in the black/in the red   loan officer
> overdraw/overdraft (facility)   penalties/penalise

1 Every month Ben Mellor earns €1,000 but spends €1,200. He _____ his account and is always _____ .
2 Ben uses his overdraft to _____ his expenses.
3 If Ben doesn't apply for an overdraft, the bank will _____ him.
4 Every month, Hana Stevens earns €1,200 and spends €1,000. She has no _____ problems. She always stays _____ .
5 If she needs more money, Hana can _____ an overdraft or personal loan. She will agree the overdraft or loan with a(n) _____ at her bank. A(n) _____ overdraft isn't very expensive.
6 Hana pays her loan in _____ .

Listening

2 ▶ 🔊 **10** Listen to Caroline, a trainee retail banker, asking her manager some questions about a customer's account. What is the problem and what is the solution?

3 Listen again and answer these questions.

1 When does Mr Müller overdraw his account?
2 What does Mr Müller have to do to be in the black?
3 What does Mr Müller have to pay when he is over his limit?
4 Why is his overdraft expensive?

Language

Modals for obligation, necessity and prohibition	
Obligation, necessity and lack of necessity	He **must** pay interest. He **will have to** pay interest on the overdraft. He **doesn't have to** pay bank charges. I **need to** talk to you.
Prohibition	He **mustn't** go over the limit.

4 Use these prompts to write sentences with modals.

next week / he / talk / to his boss ✓ (necessity – future)
Next week he will have to talk to his boss.

1 I / call / the bank / about my lost credit card ✓ (necessity – present)
2 you / usually / serve / customers in the morning / ? (obligation – present)
3 you / pay / fees / when you overdraw your account ✗ (lack of necessity – present)
4 he / make / an appointment with the loan officer / ? (necessity – present)
5 we / pay / penalties on our account ✗ (lack of necessity – future)
6 he / talk / to customers in an unfriendly way. His boss is not happy with him. ✗ (prohibition – present)

Listening 5 ▶ 🔊 11 Caroline meets Mr Müller, the customer. Listen. Are these sentences *true* (T) or *false* (F)?

1 Mr Müller wants to talk to Caroline about his account. (T / F)
2 He sometimes has to wait for a customer to pay him. (T / F)
3 Mr Müller has an overdraft facility to pay his bills. (T / F)
4 The interest rates on a loan are the same as on an overdraft facility. (T / F)
5 Mr Müller likes Caroline's suggestion. (T / F)
6 Mr Müller doesn't have to talk to a loan officer because Caroline has the application form. (T / F)

6 Listen again and write sentences about what Mr Müller has to do.

Mr Müller has to pay interest on the overdraft amount.

Reading 7 Complete this checklist from a compliance officer for new employees with *must/mustn't* and *have to/don't have to*.

To all Customer Service and Loan Officers

As you know, we have to tighten regulations, so here are some DOs and DON'Ts:

- Customer Service Officers (1) _____ contact their clients once a year.
- Customer Service Officers (2) _____ pass on personal data about their customers.
- Customer Service Officers (3) _____ arrange mortgages.
- Loan Officers (4) _____ check credit ratings before arranging loans.
- Loan Officers (5) _____ regularly write reports about existing loans.
- Loan Officers (6) _____ check financial documents of corporate clients once a year.
- Loan Officers (7) _____ make sure that the customer can pay the instalments.
- Loan Officers (8) _____ inform the guarantor of the loan when a customer is late with payments.
- Loan Officers (9) _____ approve loans before the guarantor signs the contract.

A **compliance officer** makes sure everything is done correctly.
A **guarantor** guarantees a loan.

Writing 8 You are a manager and have to do end-of-year assessments for employees. You have the information in 1–5 below from the compliance officer at the bank. Read the checklist in 7 again and write your comments after the statements.

Stefan normally contacts his clients once a month.
Stefan doesn't have to contact them once a month but he must contact them once a year.

1 George checks financial documents of corporate clients every two years.
2 Julia sometimes checks the customers' credit ratings after arranging loans.
3 George occasionally does not make sure that the customer can pay the instalments.
4 Stefan sometimes gives his customers' addresses to people outside the bank.
5 Julia occasionally forgets to write a report about an existing loan.

Speaking 9 Work in pairs. Tell Stefan, George and Julia what they need to, do not need to, must or mustn't do.

Stefan, you don't need to contact your clients once a month but you must contact them once a year.

10 Work in pairs. Talk about things you have/need to, do not have/need to, must or mustn't do at your workplace or place of study.

In my job/studies I have to … . I don't need to … . I must/mustn't … .

Mortgages

Speaking   **1**   Work in pairs. In your country, how do people get money to buy a flat or a house? Do they borrow it from a bank or a building society? Does this loan have a special name or special terms? Discuss.

Reading   **2**   Complete this mortgage application form with the words in the box.

down payment (AmE)
= deposit (BrE)

| borrow   collateral   house or flat   interest and capital |
| maturity date   property valuation   variable |

FOR SALE

MORTGAGE APPLICATION
1. The amount of the mortgage: how much do you want to _____?
2. You will need to make a deposit. What can you arrange as _____ for the bank to have some security?
3. Why you need the money: are you buying a(n) _____?
4. When will the (4) _____ be – in 25 or 30 years?
5. Do you want a fixed interest rate or a(n) _____ interest rate?
6. Do you want to pay interest only or _____?
7. Do you want to have a(n) _____?

3   Look at the application form in 2 again. Are these sentences *true* (T) or *false* (F)?

1. Customers may not choose the maturity date of the mortgage. (T / F)
2. Customers may choose variable or fixed rates. (T / F)
3. Customers may not arrange to pay interest only. (T / F)
4. Customers may arrange to have a property valuation. (T / F)
5. Customers have to give the bank something as security to get a loan. (T / F)

Language

Modals for possibility and permission	
We use *may* or *might* + infinitive to talk about possibility in the present or future.	We *may* talk to our banker about a mortgage. He *might not* get the mortgage. It is not certain.
We use *may* + infinitive to talk about permission. We use *may* or *can I/we* + infinitive to ask for permission and *may not* + infinitive to refuse permission.	Customers *may* choose their methods of payment. *Can* I speak to you? You *may not* overdraw your account.

4   Complete this conversation between a client (C) and a financial adviser (FA) with modal verbs from the Language box.

C: We would like to borrow a large amount of money – about €175,000.
FA: (1) _____ I ask why?
C: We don't have much money but we want to buy a flat.
FA: Without a deposit, a building society (2) _____ give you a mortgage. However, a bank or building society (3) _____ lend you up to €100,000 without one.
C: A €100,000 mortgage? That (4) _____ be enough to buy a flat.
FA: You (5) _____ borrow more than you can pay back, I'm afraid.
C: Can you email us more details?
FA: Certainly. (6) _____ I have your email address, please?

Speaking   **5**   Work in pairs. Talk about the pros and cons in the application form in 2.

If a customer arranges a mortgage with us, he or she may ...

Review

Language **1** Choose the correct words in italics.

1 If I *spend / will spend* too much money, I will not be able to pay it back.
2 If you have a pre-paid card, you *must / can* pay for different things with it.
3 When I need money in another country, I *look / will look* for a cash dispenser.
4 I will call the credit card company if I *have / will have* questions about my bill.
5 Can you use a debit card when you *are / will be* in another country?

2 Complete these sentences with modal verbs.

1 If you borrow money to buy a house, you _____ pay it back every month. (obligation)
2 Customers who have a mortgage with us _____ choose fixed or variable interest rates. (permission)
3 A short-term loan _____ be cheaper than an overdraft. (possibility)
4 You _____ decide today about the loan. (lack of necessity)

Vocabulary **3** Match 1–7 to a–g to make word partnerships.

1	apply	a)	a balance
2	withdraw	b)	online
3	choose	c)	for a loan
4	shop	d)	money
5	set	e)	money onto a pre-paid card
6	carry	f)	a credit limit
7	load	g)	a variable interest rate

4 Complete these sentences with the word partnerships from 3.

1 I may use my card to _____ and buy goods from a website.
2 With my PIN code and my multi-function card I can _____ from cash dispensers everywhere.
3 It is cheaper if you don't _____ from one month to the next but choose the debit option.
4 The bank uses the credit rating to _____ for a customer.
5 Parents can _____ for their children to take with them when they travel.
6 When customers arrange a mortgage, they can _____ or a fixed interest rate.
7 If you need money, you can _____ at your bank.

Speaking **5** Work in pairs. Student A, look at the information on this page. Student B, look at the information on page 71. Follow the instructions.

Student A
1 You work in banking. Student B wants to apply for a mortgage. Look at A and ask questions to get the information you need to fill in the form.
2 Swap roles. You want to apply for a credit card. Student B is the banker. Look at B and answer Student B's questions.

A

Type of property: _____
Cost of property: _____
Amount of deposit: _____
Collateral: _____
Maturity date: _____
Interest (fixed or variable): _____
Interest only or capital and interest? _____

B

- monthly salary: £1,800
- travel abroad, make purchases on the internet
- would like to use ATMs in different countries
- want a card with insurance
- want to carry a balance
- would like to load money onto card

4

Islamic banking

- explain the regulations of Islamic banking
- talk about past habits using *used to*
- express what you were trying to do
- explain different products found in Islamic banking
- compare Islamic and non-Islamic banking

The basics of Islamic banking

Speaking **1** Work in pairs. Are the sentences in this quiz *true* (T) or *false* (F)? Discuss. Give a reason for your answers.

I think this is true/correct/incorrect because ...
I am not sure but I think ...

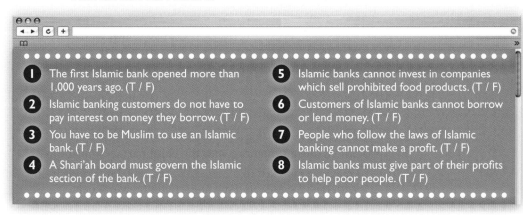

1 The first Islamic bank opened more than 1,000 years ago. (T / F)

2 Islamic banking customers do not have to pay interest on money they borrow. (T / F)

3 You have to be Muslim to use an Islamic bank. (T / F)

4 A Shari'ah board must govern the Islamic section of the bank. (T / F)

5 Islamic banks cannot invest in companies which sell prohibited food products. (T / F)

6 Customers of Islamic banks cannot borrow or lend money. (T / F)

7 People who follow the laws of Islamic banking cannot make a profit. (T / F)

8 Islamic banks must give part of their profits to help poor people. (T / F)

Reading **2** Your bank has just opened an Islamic department. You are attending a seminar on the Islamic sector. Read this text and check your answers in 1.

Facts about Islamic banking

The concept of Islamic banking started during the time of the prophet Muhammad (PBUH) and grew from the idea of Riba. This meant that people could not earn money if they lent money to others. The first Islamic bank began to operate in 1963 in Egypt. Later, in 1975, the first modern Islamic commercial bank opened in Dubai. Now there are Islamic banks all over the world.

Islamic banking follows the laws of Shari'ah (Islamic law). Banks may not charge interest on loans. Islamic banking is not only for Muslims – anyone can use a bank which follows these laws. Banks can create one section to deal with Islamic banking but they must have a Shari'ah supervisory board to make sure the section follows all the laws.

Ethical values are important at Islamic banks. Banks may not do business with companies which sell prohibited food products. Islamic banks offer the same standard products as non-Islamic banks. These include savings accounts and loans. However, an Islamic bank does not charge interest and customers do not earn it on savings. Instead, banks give a gift to customers who have accounts. This is called 'Hibah' and represents part of the profits made by the bank. Islamic law does not restrict trade, and customers can make profits when they invest. Another important aspect of Islamic banking is to give money to help others. Islamic banks must donate part of their profits to a Zakat Fund. This fund helps poor people.

Language

Listening 3 ▶ 💿 12 Complete this lecture transcript with the correct past simple form of the verbs in brackets. Then listen and check your answers.

Good afternoon, everyone. How much (1) _____ (you / know) about Islamic banking before the seminar this morning? Now you are going to hear about our new section for Islamic banking. The idea for interest-free banking (2) _____ (begin) during the time of the prophet Muhammad. People (3) _____ (not be) allowed to charge or receive interest. However, for years customers (4) _____ (not be) able to find Islamic banks. Many customers (5) _____ (ask) us about interest-free banking and other products. So we (6) _____ (decide) to open a section for these customers. First we (7) _____ (need) a Shari'ah board because the banking laws (8) _____ (have to) follow Islamic economic policies. This board (9) _____ (explain) to us how everything (10) _____ (work). Finally, we (11) _____ (offer) our first interest-free accounts to customers. We have many other products as well and you will hear about them in tomorrow's seminar.

Vocabulary 4 Match 1–7 to a–g to make word partnerships. Then match the word partnerships to definitions i–vii. Look at the texts in 2 and 3 to help you.

1	offer	a)	business	i)	not allow a business activity
2	follow	b)	trade	ii)	buy or sell services
3	create	c)	interest-free banking	iii)	do what the authorities tell you to do
4	do	d)	money	iv)	lend money but not charge for the loan
5	charge	e)	one section	v)	receive money
6	restrict	f)	laws	vi)	start one area in a company
7	earn	g)	interest	vii)	ask for money when you lend it

Speaking 5 Work in pairs. The seminar has finished for today. Talk about what you learnt. Use words from 4 and from the texts in 2 and 3.

Did you know that ...?
I didn't know that ...

The most interesting part for me was ...
What did you think about ...?

Islamic retail products

1 Complete these index cards for a presentation about different types of Islamic bank account with the correct form of the verbs in the boxes.

A

Wadiah
(Current and deposit accounts)

> guarantee   keep
> offer   receive

Islamic banking (1) _____ current and deposit accounts. The bank promises to (2) _____ the money safe for customers. It also (3) _____ a refund of the whole amount of money if the customers want it. Customers may (4) _____ a gift called 'Hibah' for allowing the bank to use the funds. If customers overdraw their account, they have to pay a fee but no interest. Both these accounts usually offer ATM cards.

B

Mudarabah
(Fixed-term deposit account)

> earn   give   have   invest

Banks also (1) _____ fixed-term deposit accounts. With these, the customer usually (2) _____ more than with a normal deposit account. The bank (3) _____ the customer's money. Then the bank (4) _____ the customer the profits from the investment. This is called profit and loss sharing or PLS. It can also be used for corporate clients as venture capital.

C

Qard hassan
(Non-profit loan)

> ask   give   make   pay

A bank (1) _____ a loan to a customer as goodwill. The borrower (2) _____ back only the amount borrowed. The borrower can (3) _____ an extra payment as thanks. The bank may (4) _____ for a service charge.

D

Ijarah with diminishing Musharaka
(Reducing partnership)

> buy   own   pay   sell

This is like a mortgage. The bank (1) _____ an asset (such as a flat) and rents it to the customer for a certain time. The bank (2) _____ the item at the beginning. Every time the customer (3) _____ some of the money back, it reduces the amount the bank owns. The customer pays a fixed rate for the time period and can (4) _____ the property if he or she pays the bank back first. The customer doesn't pay a penalty for early repayment but has to pay about 20 percent of the original value.

E

Ijarah Thumma Al Bai'
(Hire purchase)

> buy   can   lease   pay

The bank (1) _____ an asset (such as a car) for a customer. The customer (2) _____ the asset from the bank. When this contract is over, the customer (3) _____ buy the asset at a fixed price. The fixed price is higher than the original price because the customer (4) _____ the money back over a longer time.

F

Sukuk
(Islamic bonds)

> invest   mature
> prohibit   receive

As Islamic law (1) _____ the paying of interest, Islamic bonds pay only a share of profits. The bank (2) _____ in an asset or enterprise which earns money and sells bonds which represent ownership. When the bond (3) _____, the person who holds the bond (4) _____ the current value of the asset or enterprise, not the capital he or she invested.

---

2 Work in small groups. Look at the index cards in 1 again and answer these questions.

1 Which products help the customer to buy something if he or she needs money?
2 Which product helps customers to save money for a longer time?
3 Which product is an investment?
4 Which product does a customer use to buy a house or flat?
5 Which products does a customer use to manage their everyday money?

3 Now choose one account type from 1 and explain it to your group. The other members must guess which one it is.

Customers use this account in order to ...

Vocabulary   **4**   Match phrases 1–8 to definitions a–h.

1   prohibit interest
2   share a profit or a loss
3   pay a penalty
4   purchase an asset
5   reduce a percentage

6   ask for a service charge

7   lease an asset

8   guarantee a refund

a)   give money to someone to use something
b)   charge a fee
c)   buy something valuable
d)   make a part of something smaller
e)   say that to pay or receive interest is not allowed
f)   divide money which was made or lost
g)   promise to give money back to someone
h)   give extra money to someone if you did not follow the laws

Listening   **5**   ▶ 🎧 13   Abdul Farak used to use a non-Islamic bank but he is now a customer of First Bank. Listen to Mr Farak talking about the differences and complete this table.

	Non-Islamic bank	Islamic bank
Deposit account	received (1) _____ on savings	pays a(n) (4) _____ on overdraft but no interest
Current account	• received interest • paid interest if he (2) _____ his account	earns money if bank makes a(n) (5) _____
Loans	paid interest and (3) _____ every month	doesn't have a loan at the moment
Mortgage	did not want to pay interest over a long period of time	gave bank a(n) (6) _____ and bank rents the house to him

Language

Used to

We use **used to** + infinitive to talk about actions that happened regularly in the past but do not happen now.	Before we opened this section, the customers **used to ask** us about Islamic products.
We use **did (not)** + **use to** + infinitive for questions and negatives.	**Did** you **use to go** to an Islamic bank? No, I **didn't use to go** to an Islamic bank.

6   Put the words in the correct order to make sentences and questions.

1   What did he use to ask his bank about?
   used to / Islamic banking / ask his bank about / products / he
2   his account / why / did / overdraw / use to / he / ?
   He used to overdraw his account to pay the bills.
3   What didn't you use to know about?
   use to / I / Islamic banking / know about / didn't
4   deposit account / earn / what / did / she / use to / on / her?
   She used to earn interest on her deposit account.

Speaking   **7**   Work in pairs. Look at the table in 5 and make sentences about what Mr Farak used to do at the non-Islamic bank.

   When Mr Farak went to a non-Islamic bank, he used to receive ...

Writing   **8**   What did you use to do at school or at work? Write three sentences. Then compare your sentences with a partner.

   I used to ... but now I ...

Islamic corporate banking products

NEW HOTEL FINANCED WITH MUSHARAKA (JOINT VENTURE)

Two companies contributed to this joint venture, which began in ...

Speaking 1 Discuss the newspaper photo and headline. Why do you think two companies financed it together? What do you know about joint ventures?

Vocabulary 2 Complete these sentences about corporate Islamic banking with the words in the box.

| contribute | finance | instalments | lend | loses | middleman |
| purchase | shares | | | | |

1 Customers came to us because they were looking for a way to _____ a project.
2 When the bank buys an asset for a customer, it acts as a(n) _____ .
3 In a joint venture, each partner has to _____ capital to the project.
4 Customers have to pay back the money in _____ .
5 Leasing is a very common way for companies to _____ goods they need.
6 Banks often _____ money to their customers for different things.
7 If an asset _____ value, the bank _____ the risk.

buyer
↕
middleman
↕
seller

Reading 3 Read the leaflet about corporate products and answer these questions.

1 Najib buys and sells goods. Which product is best for him?
2 Leila wants to find a partner for her business. Which product is best for her?
3 Akim needs a loan to expand his business. Which product is best for him?

Musharaka (Joint venture)
• It is for business partnerships.
• Each partner contributes capital to the project.
• The bank and the customer share the profits or losses (PLS product).
• It helps companies to finance projects.

Mudarabah (Venture capital)
• Banks lend money to the customer for a business.
• The bank and the customer share the profits or losses (PLS product).
• The agreement is over when the customer pays the money back.

Murabahah (Cost plus)
• The bank acts as a middleman.
• The bank purchases the asset for the customer and sells it to the customer at a higher price.
• The customer pays the money back to the bank in instalments.
• It is also risky for the bank if the asset loses value.
• It is a type of leasing, the most common way to purchase assets and goods.

FIRST BANK

Listening   4   ▶ 🔊 14   Listen to three customers talking about their needs and match speakers 1–3 to the form of financing which would be best for each customer (a–c). Use the information in the leaflet in 3 to help you.

a) Murabahah (Cost plus) ____
b) Musharaka (Joint venture) ____
c) Mudarabah (Venture capital) ____

Language

Past continuous	
We use the **past continuous** to talk about an action or situation that was in progress at a particular time in the past. The action started before that time and continued after that time.	They **were looking** for some Islamic banking products. **Was** he **talking** to the loan adviser at 3 p.m.? Yes, he **was**./No, he **wasn't**.
We also use the **past continuous** to talk about a longer action which is stopped or interrupted by a shorter action (using *when*).	I **was reading** this leaflet **when** I found this information.

5   Complete these sentences with the correct past continuous form of the verbs in the box.

charge	do	help	look	not pay	talk	try	work

1 I _____ for a new bank when I found one which offered Islamic products.
2 My old bank _____ very high interest on my overdraft. That is why I paid it back and closed the account.
3 He _____ his instalments back regularly, so the bank sent him a letter to ask about the problem.
4 He _____ a customer when I came into his office.
5 What _____ (you) yesterday at 1 p.m.? I phoned but you weren't in.
6 We _____ to get information about Islamic products when we found an expert to help us.
7 I _____ to my manager when you phoned.
8 _____ (she) at 3 p.m. on Wednesday?

Speaking   6   Work in pairs. Write two more questions each, using the past continuous. Then take turns asking the questions.

What were you doing at 5 p.m. yesterday?
Who were you talking to when the teacher came in today?

The concepts of Islamic banking

Reading **1** UBH Bank is opening a section on Islamic banking and its employees are attending a webinar. Read their conversation and answer these questions.

1 Why couldn't Islamic customers use the normal products?
2 Why couldn't Islamic banks charge interest?
3 Why were investments as risky for the customer as for the bank?
4 What did Islamic banks have to do with some of their profits?
5 What types of companies couldn't Islamic banks invest in?

Alba:	Why did we have to open a new section of the bank? Couldn't Muslim customers use some of our products?
Kasim:	No, because we had to charge them interest. This meant they were looking for another bank to go to. We wanted to keep these customers, so we opened this section. And some non-Muslim customers are also interested in these products.
Alba:	Can you explain the background to us? How did Islamic banking begin?
Kasim:	The ideas came from Islamic law. One idea is co-operation. For example, when someone invested in a company, they made money when the company did well. If it didn't do well, they lost money. This way, the investor and the company shared the risks and the bank didn't have to pay the investor interest, only part of the profits.
Alba:	I see. Anything else?
Kasim:	Yes, Islamic law did not allow Riba, which is charging someone to use your money. So Islamic banks don't charge interest, only fees.
Matthew:	But aren't fees as expensive as interest for customers?
Kasim:	Not usually. And other products use the PLS or 'profit and loss sharing' idea. This means investments or savings accounts are as risky for the customers as for the bank.
Katja:	That's interesting. Are there other important ideas?
Kasim:	Oh yes. For example, when Islamic banking began, banks had to give some of their profits to charity. We still do that today. They also have to assess their clients and must work only with ethical ones. They are not allowed to invest in companies that sell prohibited food products, for example.
Alba:	So the ideas behind Islamic banking were not just offering interest-free accounts ...

Language

Modals in the past

We use **could** for things we were able to or allowed to do in the past.	**Could** customers use our products? No, they **couldn't**.
We use **had to** for things that were necessary and **didn't have to** for things that were unnecessary.	**Did** you **have to** look for a new bank? Yes, we **had to** look for a bank where we **didn't have to** pay interest.

3 Complete these sentences with modal verbs from the Language box.

1 We _____ to phone our bank about the agreement. (it was necessary)
2 My clients were very happy they _____ take out an interest-free loan with us. (were able to)
3 _____ (you) tell him about the new products? (was it necessary?)
4 They _____ pay a fee. (it was not necessary)
5 _____ the bank find another company to invest in? (was it able to?)

34   4 | Islamic banking

Review

1 Complete these sentences with the words in the box.

capital	charity	co-operation	hire	purchases	refund	represent	sharing

1 The bank guarantees a _____ of all the money customers deposit.
2 Islamic banks have profit and loss _____ products.
3 Customers can buy goods using a _____ purchase system.
4 Islamic bonds _____ real assets or enterprises.
5 The money someone puts into an investment is called _____ .
6 Islamic banks give part of their profits to _____ .
7 One very important part of Islamic banking is _____ .
8 The bank _____ an asset for a customer and then sells it to him or her.

2 Match words 1–6 to their opposites a–f. Then work in pairs. Take turns to make sentences using one word from each pair.

1 borrow   a) spend
2 prohibit   b) withdraw
3 deposit   c) loss
4 save   d) pay
5 receive   e) allow
6 profit   f) lend

A: I deposit money into my account.
B: I need money, so I withdraw it from the ATM.

Language **3** Read this email and choose the correct words in *italics*.

Dear Sue,
We (1) *had / were having* a very interesting seminar last week. Our bank opened a new section for Islamic banking and we (2) *had to / didn't have to* learn about it – the new section is as important as the rest of the bank. Before we offered Islamic products, customers (3) *can't / couldn't* get interest-free accounts. Last month some customers (4) *thought / were thinking* about looking for another bank when they (5) *found out / were finding out* about our new section. So they (6) *stayed / were staying* with us. It was a great chance to learn about these new products. I think you will find this interesting as well.

Writing **4** Continue the email in 3. Include three things that you learnt and three things that you found really interesting.

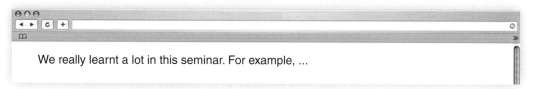

We really learnt a lot in this seminar. For example, ...

Speaking **5** Work in pairs. Student A, look at the information on page 68. Student B, look at the information on page 71. Follow the instructions.

5

The structure of a bank

- describe the work in different departments of a bank
- talk about banking jobs, responsibilities and tasks
- explain the hierarchy in a bank
- talk about change

Departments

Reading

Atlantic Banking Group

Board of Directors	Human Resources	Retail Banking
Private Banking	Corporate Banking	Loan Modification
Foreign Exchange	Group Accounting	Internal Audit
Group Risk	Client Risk Management	Legal Department

1 Read this brochure about jobs in a bank. Match six of the departments above to the employees.

(1) _____
'I deal with customers who have large amounts to invest. We are in charge of managing investment portfolios and giving investment advice.' (Leila)

(2) _____
'I report directly to the Board of Directors about risks within the bank. My department prepares the annual risk report and we help to decide on future strategies.' (Elke)

(3) _____
'In my department we are involved in creating tailor-made products and advising corporate clients.' (Grete)

(4) _____
'I deal with large companies. I check on the collateral they have and I check their credit ratings to make sure we can lend them money.' (Duncan)

(5) _____
'We are responsible for doing the books and preparing the financial documents.' (David)

(6) _____
'I deal with exchange rates and foreign currencies. We help customers when they want to change money.' (Susan)

Speaking

2 Work in pairs. Match the rest of the departments above to these sentences.

1 We are responsible for recruiting and training staff as well as paying employees. _____
2 Customers come here to make a bank transfer or ask a question about their account. They can also open or close their account. _____
3 We help corporate customers when they have financial difficulties and take care of modifying loans and credit lines. _____
4 We deal with legal problems and lawsuits. _____
5 We check on the work in other departments. We are in charge of making sure everything is done correctly. _____
6 We are in charge of running the bank. We look at all the information and plan long-term strategies. The managers of the other departments report to us.
_____

3 Work in pairs. Find the nouns used with these verbs in 1 and 2. Then take turns to make questions using the verb–noun partnerships for your partner to guess the department.

change	check on	create	decide on	do	give	manage
modify	prepare	recruit	report to			

A: Who creates tailor-made products?
B: Corporate Banking (does).

Language

Prepositions	
Some verbs, verb phrases and adjectives take specific prepositions (e.g. *deal with, report to, look at, check on, be in charge of, take care of, be involved in, be responsible for*).	*They **are in charge of** managing investment portfolios.* *He **takes care of** corporate customers.* *I **am involved in** training courses.* *My department **checks on** the collateral.*
Prepositions are followed by a noun, pronoun or gerund.	*I deal **with exchange rates**.* *We are responsible **for running** the whole bank.*

4 Choose the correct words in *italics*.

1 I take care *to / of* tailor-made products for corporate clients. _____

2 I am responsible *to audit / for auditing* the books of the bank. I have to make sure that everything we do is correct. _____

3 I help my boss *with / at* the preparation of financial documents for the bank. _____

4 We are in charge *to modify / of modifying* corporate loans when customers have cash flow problems. We help them to pay their loans back.
_____

5 We deal *with / for* managing investment portfolios for wealthy customers.
_____

6 My department is in charge *to recruit / of recruiting* new staff members. We also train existing staff to help them do their jobs better.
_____

Listening **5** ▶ 🎧 **15** Write the name of the department for each sentence in 4. Then listen and check your answers.

Speaking **6** Work in pairs. Ask your partner what he or she does, did or will do at work. Use the verbs in the box to help you.

audit	be in charge of	be responsible for	change	check on
create	deal with	decide on	give	manage	open and close
plan	prepare	recruit and train	report to	take care of

A: What are you responsible for?
B: I'm responsible for recruiting and training new staff.

The structure of the bank

Atlantic Banking Group – an overview

1 The Retail Banking Department is responsible for the everyday banking needs of individual customers. ___
2 The Human Resources Department is in charge of hiring new staff. ___
3 The Corporate Banking Department deals with companies. ___
4 The Internal Audit Department checks on procedures throughout the bank. ___
5 The Training Department is involved in organising training, and reports to the Human Resources Director. ___
6 The Client Risk Department deals with corporate customers and assesses their ability to repay loans. ___
7 The Group Accounting Department is responsible for preparing the bank's accounts. ___
8 The Group Risk Department reports to the Chief Risk Officer and is responsible for assessing risks for the whole bank. ___

a) This department looks at companies' financial documents and assesses the risk involved in giving loans.
b) Employees in this department audit the books and the other departments. They make sure everyone is working correctly.
c) The people in this department try to find out what the other employees need to learn. Then they set up training courses.
d) Employees in this department advise clients to set up credit lines. They also work to create special products for their clients.
e) The people in this department get information from the bank's accounting systems. They help to prepare all the financial documents for the Board of Directors.
f) This department recruits new employees.
g) This department looks at individual customers' financial documents. They assess each of them according to the risks of the products and the economy.
h) Employees in this department spend their time opening current and deposit accounts, arranging small loans, setting up overdraft facilities and doing everyday banking business.

2 Look at the organogram and descriptions in 1 again. Answer these questions.

1 Which department works with all the people at the bank?
2 Which department makes sure all the departments work correctly?
3 Which department works with medium-sized and large companies?
4 Which department is in charge of assessing risk for the whole bank?

Language

Gerund or infinitive after a verb	
Some verbs and verb phrases are followed by a **gerund**.	*We consider/are involved in/suggest/risk **giving** loans.* *I don't mind/enjoy/spend time **talking** to customers.*
Some verbs are followed by an **infinitive with to**.	*They agreed/arranged/decided/helped/offered/prepared/ refused/wanted/tried **to set up** an overdraft.*
Some verbs are followed by an **object + infinitive with to**.	*They advise/allow/help/permit/recommend/want **customers to invest** in funds.* *They expect/ask/recommend/require/want **customers to have** good credit ratings.*

3 Work in pairs. Interview your partner using the language from the Language box. Note down his/her answers and report back to the class.

What are you involved in doing at work/school?

Vocabulary **4** Look at this organogram and complete the sentences with the words in the box.

> above   below   on the same level   report to   supervises

1 There is a director _____ the managers.
2 There are several employees _____ the managers.
3 The employees _____ the managers.
4 The three managers are _____ .
5 The director _____ the managers.

Listening **5** ▶ 🎧 16   Now listen to Ali, Jo, Dan and Sarah talking about their departments and check your answers in 4.

6 Listen again and match the speakers to these sentences. Write the correct name next to each sentence.

1 This person finds out what people in other departments need. _____
2 This person works with companies. _____
3 This person works with customers at a branch. _____
4 This person has to check on other departments. _____
5 This person considers loans for large businesses. _____
6 This person has someone to help him/her. _____

Speaking **7** Work in pairs. Student A, look at the information on page 69. Student B, look at the information on page 72. Follow the instructions.

Presentation skills

Vocabulary **1** Work in pairs. Label the illustration with words 1–8.

1 remote control	4 screen	7 laptop
2 data projector	5 laser pointer	8 slide
3 handouts	6 index cards	

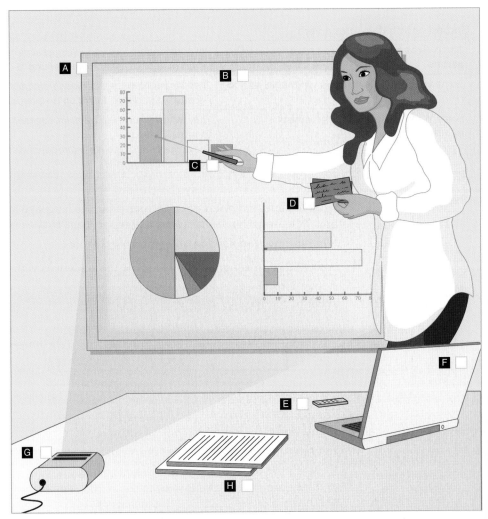

2 Match 1–9 to a–i to make sentences and phrases often used in presentations.

1 Good morning and welcome
2 My name is
3 This presentation will have
4 In the first part I am going
5 Then we are going to move
6 Finally we are going to
7 You are welcome to
8 I would like to finish by

9 Thank you all

a) to tell you about …
b) conclude with …
c) on to …
d) for coming today.
e) summing up the main points.
f) to my presentation.
g) three parts.
h) Bob Jones and I am going to talk about …
i) ask questions.

Speaking **3** Work in pairs or small groups. Use the sentences and phrases in 2 to talk about yourself or your company.

My name is Ahmed Al-Shebani and I am going to talk about jobs in the bank.

4 You are going to listen to a talk. Put these signposting phrases in the order you think you will hear them. The first three sentences belong to the introduction. The last seven belong to the main part and the conclusion of the presentation.

☐ My presentation is in three parts. ☐ Thank you for your attention.
☐ The last part is going to be about ... ☐ Now moving on to ...
☐ Good morning everyone. ☐ To sum up, ...
☐ In conclusion, ... ☐ Finally, ...
☐ So to start off, ... ☐ Are there any questions?

5 ▶ 🔊 **17** Listen and check your answers in 4.

Speaking

6 Work in pairs. Discuss these questions. Listen to track 17 again if necessary.

profit margin = difference between interest paid on accounts and interest paid on loans

1 How do banks use the money from customers' deposit accounts?
2 What is the difference between an overdraft facility and a credit line?
3 What can the bank calculate with loans?
4 What type of rates does the bank offer for loans?
5 How does a bank calculate its profit margin?

Language

Future forms and past simple

We use **be going to** or the **present continuous** to outline a plan for a talk.	*I **am going to tell** you about our new banking products.* *We **are introducing** new regulations next week.*
We use the **past simple** to summarise what we covered in a talk.	*I **explained** our new banking products.* *I **told** you about the new regulations.*

7 Use these prompts to write sentences using *going to*. Then rewrite the sentences using the present continuous.

1 you / talk / to your boss / tomorrow / ?
2 he / give / a presentation / next week
3 we / not recruit / new staff / this year
4 I / change / departments / next year
5 they / modify / the loan for the client / ?

Speaking

8 Work in pairs. Choose a topic and outline your plan for a talk. Tell your partner what you are going to say about it. Use at least four sentences. Then swap roles and repeat the activity.

I am going to talk about ...
Then I am going to ...

9 Work in pairs. Find out what your partner's problem is. What is he/she going to do about it? Listen and give advice. Then swap roles and repeat the activity.

Student A
You work in the Group Accounting Department. You enjoy working with customers and in this job you only see your colleagues. You would like to change your job. Talk to your partner about what you are going to do.

Student B
You work at a branch where you serve customers every day. You like your job but you really enjoy working in a quieter environment. You would like to change to another department. Talk to your partner about what you are going to do.

10 Work with a new partner. Tell him/her about the outcome of your discussion in 9.

The changing world of banking

Reading **1** Work in pairs. Discuss changes in your own banks.

My bank used to ... but it doesn't any longer.

2 Read this text about banking. Are these sentences *true* (T), *false* (F) or is there *no information* in the text (NI)?

1 Modern-day banking began in the fifteenth century. ___
2 Retail banks have existed for more than 300 years. ___
3 In the seventeenth century English people used the receipts they got from their banks to buy gold and silver. ___
4 Banks have opened branches in supermarkets around the world. ___
5 People like to use the machines in the lobby. ___
6 Banks have joined together with other banks. ___

The changing world of banking

Banking began in the twelfth century in Italy. Moneylenders set up benches in the marketplace to do transactions. In the UK retail banking started in the seventeenth century. People began to use banks to keep their gold and silver safe. The bank gave them receipts, and customers used these as currency.

Today many of the early banks have expanded into financial supermarkets for customers. They offer current and deposit accounts and make payments through EFTPOS (electronic funds transfer at point of sale) in shops and restaurants. In addition, they issue credit cards, pre-paid cards, debit cards and smart cards. Many banks even give financial advice and sell insurance and pension plans.

Even the methods of banking have changed. People used to use cheques widely. Today most customers use direct debits or standing orders to pay their bills. Many customers open online accounts. This means that they no longer have to come into the bank. And when they do, they usually use the machines in the lobby and they don't speak with a banker at all. It is much more difficult today for bankers to get to know their customers. It is also harder to advise them or sell them other products.

This is why banks have come up with other ways to meet their customers. World Savings Day was started in 1924 in Milan, Italy but is now expanding to countries where people sometimes don't use banks at all. The banks give their customers gifts for opening savings accounts. Sometimes they hold events or invite customers to come to them to hear about investments or other financial topics.

Today many banks have become larger and have merged with other banks. Customers no longer know the people that they deal with. That is one reason why banks are trying to find new ways to win customers.

Language

Present perfect

Present perfect	
We use the **present perfect** to talk about actions which started in the past and have not finished, or which happened in the past and have an effect on the present. To form the present perfect, we use *have/has* + past participle.	*Early banks **have expanded** into financial supermarkets.*
We use *for* for a period of time and **since** for a fixed point in time.	*Banks **have existed for** over 300 years.* *Banks **have changed** greatly **since** those times.*
We use *ever* in questions. We use a form of **have** in short answers.	***Have** you **ever worked** in an investment bank?* *Yes, I **have**./No, I **haven't**.*

Speaking **3** Work in pairs. Write three statements each, using the present perfect. Two are correct, one is false. Your partner guesses which one is false.

I have been to Japan. I have never been to the US. I have worked in the UK.

Review

Language **1** Complete these sentences with *be going to*, the present perfect, a gerund or an infinitive.

    1 I _____ (manage) portfolios for wealthy clients since I began working here.

    2 My department is responsible for _____ (take) care of corporate clients.

    3 Last week I helped my boss _____ (check on) the credit ratings of our clients.

    4 Next week Group Accounting _____ (prepare) the financial documents for the Managing Director.

    5 He _____ (be) a client of mine for many years.

    6 I spend my time _____ (serve) customers at the branch.

    7 We _____ (talk) to a corporate customer this afternoon about a new product.

    8 We don't usually risk _____ (lend) money to customers we don't know.

    9 We are in charge of _____ (recruit) new staff for the bank.

    10 He advised me _____ (invest) in funds.

Vocabulary **2** Match 1–8 to a–h to make word partnerships. Then match them to definitions i–viii.

1	recruit	a)	tailor-made products
2	modify	b)	the Managing Director
3	create	c)	the books
4	plan	d)	portfolios
5	audit	e)	clients
6	report to	f)	loans
7	manage	g)	long-term strategies
8	advise	h)	staff

    i)   to work directly for the person who runs the company

    ii)   to look after investments for clients

    iii) to change loans so that customers can pay them back more easily

    iv) to find and hire new employees

    v)   to decide on actions for the future

    vi) to make special products for customers

    vii) to make suggestions to customers

    viii) to check the figures in the books

Speaking **3** Work in pairs. Choose a topic from this unit. Use these signposting phrases and create a mini-presentation on your topic. Make the presentation to your partner. Your partner then asks you questions about your presentation.

Introduction
Good morning.
My name is ... and I am going to tell you about ...
My presentation is in ... parts.
First ...
Then ...
Finally, ...

Main part
To start off, ...
Now moving on to ...
Next ...
To sum up, ...

Conclusion
In conclusion, ...
Do you have any questions?
Thank you for your attention.

Finance in companies

- talk about cash flow in a compan[y]
- describe a balance sheet
- explain an income statement
- explain a cash flow statement

Cash flow

Vocabulary **1** Work in pairs. Match words and phrases 1–11 to definitions a–k.

1 advance ___
2 cash flow problems ___
3 change in demand ___
4 deposit ___
5 invoice ___
6 lack of cash ___
7 meet expenses ___
8 order ___
9 pay in full ___
10 put off payment ___
11 unforeseen costs ___

a) a request to supply goods or services
b) this money is often paid to reserve something
c) pay your bills
d) expenses you do not expect
e) not enough money coming in to cover expenses
f) when people or companies start needing more or less of a product or service
g) send someone a bill for work you have done
h) money you pay someone to start a job; they receive the rest at the end
i) pay bills at a later date
j) completely pay off a debt
k) when money is not available

Speaking **2** Work in pairs. Look at the newspaper headline and discuss these questions. Use the words in 1. Then compare your answers with another pair.

1 What sort of company do you think Events & Co is? Are they successful?
2 What do you think causes cash flow problems?

BUSINESS NEWS *Wednesday 1 May*

EVENTS & CO IN CASH FLOW CRISIS

Unforeseen costs and change in demand create problems for the company.

Reading **3** Read the guidelines for bank advisers and answer these questions.

billing period = how long a customer has to pay

1 What does the banker ask about billing their customers?
2 How does the bank's client get money when he or she needs it?
3 What information does the bank need to give the client a loan?

Guidelines for bank advisers: how to deal with clients' cash flow problems

- How much cash does the customer need?
- When does the customer send invoices?
- How long is the billing period?
- How often does the customer use an overdraft?
- How much does the customer pay in interest?
- How long has the company been in business?
- Has the customer always paid his/her bills?
- Does the customer have other loans?

Listening 4 ▶ 🎧 18 Work in pairs. Listen to a radio interview in which Steve Jones from Events & Co talks about cash flow in his company and answer these questions.

1 Did the company make a profit from the job he describes?
2 What were some of the problems that he had?

5 Listen again and complete this table.

	Jan	Feb	Mar	Apr	May	June	July
Income	(1) €_____	€0	€0	€0	(6) €_____	€0	(8) €_____
Expenses	(2) €_____	(3) €_____	(4) €_____	€2,500 + (5) €_____ (interest)	€3,000	(7) €_____	(9) €_____ + €375 (interest)

6 Work in pairs. Look at the audio script for track 18 on page 77 and answer these questions.

1 How much did Steve Jones get for the event?
2 How many months did he need to plan the event?
3 How much did he pay to suppliers?
4 How much did he pay in interest?
5 How much gross profit did he make?

gross profit = profit
before paying taxes

Language

Quantifiers

We use **some** with countable and uncountable nouns. We use it in affirmative sentences and questions.	They had **some** unforeseen costs. Would you like **some** coffee?
We use **any** with countable and uncountable nouns. We use it in questions and negative sentences.	Do you have **any** problems with your customers? We didn't have **any** income in April.
We use **a lot of** with countable and uncountable nouns, usually in affirmative sentences.	I've had **a lot of** expenses I didn't expect. We haven't had **a lot of** time to complete the report.
We use **many – more – the most** and (a) **few – fewer – the fewest** with countable nouns.	Does this happen with **many** customers? Yes, with **most** of them. There are **few** banks in the area.
We use **much – more – the most** and (a) **little – less – the least** with uncountable nouns.	We avoid paying so **much** interest. We had **little** time to take care of it. **Less** money came in than we thought.

7 Choose the correct words in *italics*.

1 How *many / much* money does he have in his deposit account?
2 The company is doing well and has *few / little* debts.
3 They have not received *some / any* payments for their work.
4 They have hired *some / any* companies to cater for an event.
5 I have very *few / little* time tomorrow for the meeting.
6 We had the *fewest / least* problems with our last project.

Speaking 8 Work in pairs. You run a small business. Tell your partner about a recent project. Then swap roles and repeat the activity. Talk about:

• what sort of company you run.
• the length of the project.
• how much you got for the project.
• your expenses.

The balance sheet

Reading **1** Work in pairs. Look at this balance sheet. Can you think of any other items which could come under these headings? Discuss.

Atlas Ltd				
Balance sheet – as at 5 April 2012				
Assets	**€25,639**	**Equity**		**€7,062**
Current assets	*€11,764*	Shareholders' equity		€2,860
Cash	€3,466	Retained earnings		€4,202
Accounts receivable	€4,324	**Liabilities**		**€18,577**
Inventory	€3,974			
Non-current assets	*€13,875*	*Current liabilities*		*€12,095*
Tangible assets	*€9,144*	Accounts payable		€5,517
Buildings	€6,096	Taxes		€3,822
Equipment	€3,048	Short-term loan		€2,756
Intangible assets	*€4,731*	*Non-current liabilities*		*€6,482*
Brand names	€3,154	Long-term loan		€6,482
Patents	€1,577			
Total assets	**€25,639**	**Total liabilities**		**€25,639**

2 Find words in the balance sheet in 1 that match these definitions.

1 things owned by a company _____
2 debts; money owed to someone else _____
3 things that can be quickly turned into cash _____
4 things that cannot be quickly turned into cash _____
5 money customers owe to a company _____
6 money a company owes to suppliers _____
7 finished or partially finished goods owned by a company _____
8 things that can be touched like a building or machine _____
9 things that cannot be touched like a brand name or patent _____
10 debts a company has to pay within one year _____
11 debts a company does not have to pay in the current year _____
12 money shareholders invested plus retained earnings _____
13 money a company keeps to use for the business or to pay debts _____

Speaking **3** Work in pairs. What do you know about balance sheets? Where did you learn about them? Do you deal with balance sheets in your job?

Language

Passive forms	
We form **the passive** with the correct form of *be* + past participle. We use the passive: • when the action is more important than who does it. • when it is clear who does the action. • to highlight the agent (who or what does the action) using **by**.	These assets **can be converted** into cash. The balance sheet **is divided** into two parts. The company **was invoiced** last month. (clear who did the action) The money **is paid by shareholders**. (highlights who did the action)

4 Rewrite these sentences in the passive. Use *by* only where necessary.

1 The Group Accounting Department prepares the balance sheet.
   The balance sheet _____ .
2 We can sell the asset.
   The asset _____ .
3 We add the figures together.
   The figures _____ .
4 The shareholders can provide more capital.
   More capital _____ .

5 Work in pairs. Use these prompts to ask and answer questions in the passive. Then make your own questions about banks and companies.

1 training / provide / HR
2 products / sell / Retail Banking
3 important decisions / make / Board of Directors
4 financial documents / prepare / Group Accounting
5 loans / modify / Loan Modification
6 risk / analyse / Group Risk

A: How is training provided in your company?
B: It's provided by HR.

Language

Large numbers	
When we say large numbers, we use **and** between the hundreds and the tens, including when they are multipliers. 1,000 = one thousand 100,000 = one hundred thousand 1,000,000 = one million 1,000,000,000 = one billion (one thousand million) 1,000,000,000,000 = one trillion (one million million) Note: we say *two million*, not *two millions*.	*300,461 = three hundred thousand four hundred **and** sixty-one* *34,987,125 = thirty-four million nine hundred **and** eighty-seven thousand one hundred **and** twenty-five*
Large figures can also be said with a decimal point. We use a comma to separate billions and millions, and millions and thousands. We use a point (.) for decimal points. The numbers after the decimal point are said individually.	*87,656,000,000 = eighty-seven point six five six billion* *1.75 = one point seven five*

Listening **6** ▶ 🔊 19 Work in pairs. Listen to six numbers and write them down. Then take turns to read the numbers to each other.

Speaking **7** Work in pairs. Student A, look at the information on page 69. Student B, look at the information on page 72. Follow the instructions.

The income statement

Speaking **1** Work in pairs. Choose the correct answer, a, b or c. Discuss.

1 An income statement shows
   a) how many customers a company has.
   b) how much the company needed to borrow.
   c) how much the company earned and spent.
2 The income statement is used with the balance sheet to
   a) find out about the financial position of a company.
   b) compare the figures.
   c) explain the balance sheet.
3 Numbers written in brackets show
   a) numbers from the year before.
   b) negative numbers.
   c) numbers which are estimated.

Listening **2** ▶ 🔊 **20** Listen and check your answers in 1.

Vocabulary **3** Look at the income statement for Electronics and More Ltd and match these definitions to the underlined words.

1 the gradual decrease in value of an intangible asset _____
2 the money earned before paying interest and tax _____
3 money the company earned _____
4 the amount of money spent to produce and sell a product _____
5 the amount earned for selling goods minus discounts given to customers _____
6 the gradual decrease in value for a tangible asset _____

EBIT = earnings before interest and tax
( ) = minus figure

Income statement for Electronics and More Ltd
6 April 2011 – 5 April 2012
[figures in 000s]

Operating revenues	
Sales	€8,900
Operating expenses	
Cost of goods sold	(€2,739)
Sales, General and Administrative Expenses (SG&A)	(€3,955)
Depreciation and amortisation	(€643)
Total operating costs	**(€7,337)**
Operating profit	€1,563
Non-operating profit	€0
EBIT	€1,563
Interest	(€148)
Earnings before income taxes	€1,415
Income taxes	(€369)
Net profit after tax	**€1,046**

+ plus
− minus
× times/multiplied by
= equals/is
÷ divided by
% percent

Speaking **4** Work in pairs. Look at the box of mathematical formulas above. Write down three mathematical formulas and read them to your partner. Your partner should write them down. Then swap roles and repeat the activity.

Listening **5** ▶ 🔊 **21** Your boss is explaining how the bank looks at an income statement to decide if the company can get a loan or not. Look at the income statement in 3. Listen and circle the words you hear.

6 Look again at the income statement in 3 and the income statement below. Read the audio script for tracks 20 and 21 on pages 77–78. Are these statements *true* (T), *false* (F) or is there *no information* (NI) in the text?

1 The net profit after tax is found by subtracting the operating expenses from the net sales. ___
2 Comparing the net profit margin from one year to another might show if the company has done better or not. ___
3 Last year's sales and net profit margin were lower. ___
4 Companies in the same field also produce income statements. ___
5 The income statement and the balance sheet should both be looked at. ___
6 The income statement may be less important than the balance sheet. ___

Income statement for Electronics and More Ltd

6 April 2010 – 5 April 2011
[figures in 000s]

Operating revenues	
Sales	€7,600
Net profit after tax	**€996**

Language

Modals of speculation	
We use **can**, **may**, **might** or **could** to speculate or guess.	*It **might** mean their performance is not as good as it was last year.*
We use an infinitive without *to* after **can**, **may**, **might** or **could**.	*It **could mean** that there were problems in the whole sector last year.*

7 Put the words in 1–3 in the correct order to make sentences.

1 next year / be better / may not
2 might / higher operating costs / have / they / next year
3 a lot of problems / they / have / and / might not / recover / they

Speaking **8** Work in pairs. Do you think it will be a good idea to lend Electronics and More Ltd money? Talk about the problems that could arise and the other documents you would like to look at.

It could be a problem if ...   *I would like to see ...*
We may need to ask them about ...   *It might be better to ...*

Writing **9** Write a short report about the income statement of Electronics and More Ltd for your boss. Explain how the figures were reached.

This report aims to explain the income statement of ...
Last year the company earned ... in net sales.
Their operating expenses were ...
This was a result of ... plus ...

The cash flow statement

1 Work in pairs. What do you think a cash flow statement shows? How it is different from an income statement? Look at this cash flow statement for Electronics and More Ltd and the text next to it to check your answers.

Cash flow statements are the third important document that companies produce. The income statement shows if the company made a profit and the cash flow statement shows if the company generated cash. When we look at the bottom line of the cash flow statement, we see if operations resulted in a net increase or decrease in the cash the company has. Therefore, the cash flow statement is important for finding out if the company can pay its bills.

Electronics and More Ltd – Cash flow statement

Part 1	Cash flow from operations	
	(1) Profit after tax	€300,000
	(2) Decrease in accounts receivable	€48,000
	(3) Increase in taxes payable	€43,000
	(4) Increase in accounts payable	€52,000
	(5) *Net cash from operations*	*€443,000*
Part 2	Cash flow from investing	
	(6) Plant and equipment	(€137,500)
Part 3	Cash flow from financing	
	(7) Issuing new shares	€65,000
	(8) Bank loans	€202,000
	(9) Net increase in cash	**€572,500**

Reading **2** Look at the cash flow statement in 1 again and match 1–9 to definitions a–i.

Part 1

a) The company has more cash on hand because the customers have paid their debts. ___

b) The company has more cash on hand because they are waiting to pay their taxes till a later date. ___

c) All the expenses are subtracted, resulting in this final figure. ___

d) The company has more cash on hand because they are waiting to pay suppliers till a later date. ___

e) Here we see all the cash the company generated by doing business. ___

Parts 2 and 3

f) This expense was caused by buying equipment for the factory. ___

g) This money came from a bank. ___

h) This final figure resulted from all cash movements. ___

i) This figure is a result of finding people to invest in company stock. ___

Language

Cause and effect	
To express **cause**, we use *because* or *as* + a new clause.	The PLA is important **because** investors can see the performance of a company for a period of time.
We also use phrases such as *thanks to, owing to, due to, because of* + a gerund or a noun.	The company lost money **due to** higher prices for raw materials.
To express **effect** or **result**, we use words such as *therefore* or *consequently*.	**Therefore**, the cash flow statement is important.
We also use phrases such as *result in* or *resulting in* + a gerund or a noun.	All the expenses are subtracted, **resulting in** this final figure.

3 Join these sentences using the words in brackets.

1 We had very high expenses. We have a cash flow problem. (resulting in)

2 We were late with our bank payment. We experienced a lack of demand last month. (owing to)

3 We had to invest in new machinery. We don't have much cash. (therefore)

Review

Language **1** Choose the correct words in *italics*.

1 Cash flow problems are often *caused by / resulting in* late payments from customers.
2 The company hasn't got *some / any* problems with orders for next month.
3 Our products are *manufacture / manufactured* in Europe.
4 Their lack of cash was *bringing / brought* about by the bank asking for loan repayments.
5 We have very *few / little* time to discuss the problem.
6 We *might / can* do better next year but I am not sure about it.

2 Write these mathematical formulas in words. Then work in pairs and practise saying them aloud.

1 $64{,}098 + 3{,}456 = 67{,}554$
2 $769{,}001 - 56{,}231 = 712{,}770$
3 $87{,}090 \times 65 = 5{,}660{,}850$
4 $1{,}981{,}980 \div 605 = 3{,}276$

Vocabulary **3** Work in pairs. Use the clues to unscramble these words. Then use the letters in the numbered boxes to find the secret words.

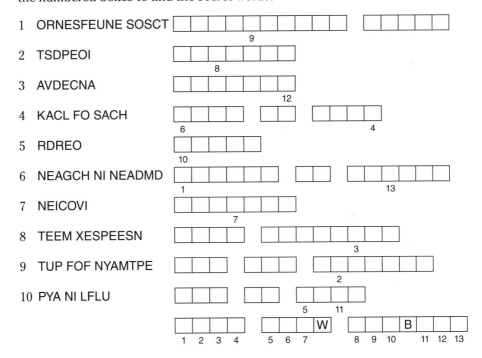

1 ORNESFEUNE SOSCT
2 TSDPEOI
3 AVDECNA
4 KACL FO SACH
5 RDREO
6 NEAGCH NI NEADMD
7 NEICOVI
8 TEEM XESPEESN
9 TUP FOF NYAMTPE
10 PYA NI LFLU

1 expenses you do not expect
2 money you pay for something at the beginning which is only part of the whole amount
3 money you pay someone when they start a job; they receive the rest when they finish.
4 when money is not available
5 a request to supply goods or services
6 when other people or companies no longer need as much of a product or service
7 send someone a bill for work they have done
8 pay bills
9 pay bills at a later date
10 completely pay off a debt

Writing **4** Work in pairs. Choose one of the documents in the unit (balance sheet, income statement or cash flow statement) and write an explanation of what it consists of and how it is used. Read it to your partner, who guesses which document you have described.

Corporate banking

- make suggestions for products for corporate clients
- find out about credit lines, corporate and leasing
- talk about loan modification and cor restructuring
- find out about bankruptcy

Taking care of corporate clients

Speaking **1** Work in pairs. Can you name three products a bank offers to corporate clients? What is it important for a bank to do before it lends money to a company?

Listening **2** ▶ 🎧 22 Marta is an intern spending the week in a corporate banking department. Listen to her conversation with the head of the department and answer these questions.

1 What is the main difference between corporate banking and retail banking?
2 What does a credit analyst do?
3 What is a risk assessment?
4 How does a bank know if a customer is creditworthy?
5 What three areas does Piotr mention as part of his new job?

Vocabulary **3** Match words 1–6 to definitions a–f.

1 letter of credit ___
2 bank draft ___
3 credit line ___
4 bank guarantee ___
5 leasing agreement ___
6 corporate bond ___

a) an arrangement by a bank to give a customer a specific amount of unsecured credit, similar to an overdraft
b) a debt security issued by a company sold to investors
c) a written promise by an importer's bank to pay the exporter's bank on a particular date or time after the goods are sent by the importer
d) a promise by a bank to pay a loan if the original borrower does not pay it back
e) a type of cheque where the payment is guaranteed because it is issued by a bank
f) an arrangement to pay to use equipment, buildings, cars, etc. rather than buying them

Vocabulary **4** Match products 1–6 to situations a–f.

1 bank draft
2 corporate bonds
3 credit line

4 letter of credit
5 bank guarantees
6 leasing agreement

a) 'I don't want to pay for goods from another country until they are shipped.'
b) 'I need a new machine for my factory.'
c) 'I want to make sure the buyer has funds to pay me.'
d) 'My company needs to raise capital.'
e) 'The bank promises to pay my debts to my suppliers if I can't.'
f) 'I need to have different amounts of cash on hand at different times.'

Listening **5** 🎧 **23** Listen to the three conversations and decide which aspect of corporate banking the people are discussing. Match the conversations (1–3) to a–c.

a) risk assessment ____
b) expansion ____
c) financing international trade ____

6 Listen again. Are these sentences *true* (T) or *false* (F)? Correct the false sentences.

1 Mr Kosnik asked the bank to get the information about the company in Jakarta. (T / F)
2 The bank is worried about Mr Ferrando's creditworthiness. (T / F)
3 Ms Park is thinking about selling some of her business. (T / F)

Language

Second conditional	
We use the **second conditional** to talk about unreal or imagined situations, to give advice or to make recommendations. We use the form: *if* + past simple + *would* + infinitive.	*If I wanted to import goods to Poland, what would I need to do?*
The *if* clause can come before or after the main clause in the sentence. When it comes at the beginning, we put a comma after it.	*We would have a better idea of your situation if you gave us your profit and loss accounts.*

7 Complete these second conditional sentences with the correct form of the verbs in brackets.

1 If a client _____ (show) me his balance sheet, I _____ (talk) to him about it.
2 I _____ (recommend) a letter of credit if a customer _____ (want) to import goods from abroad.
3 If a customer _____ (decide) to expand, I _____ (discuss) different types of financing with him or her.
4 What _____ (you / do) if a customer _____ (not pay) back a loan?
5 If a client _____ (not show) us the documents we needed, we _____ (not arrange) a credit line or loan for him.

Speaking **8** Work in pairs. Talk about what you would do in these situations. Use the second conditional.

1 Someone offers you an exciting job in London.
2 You get the opportunity to move to another country.
3 You are given the opportunity to work in the Corporate Banking Department.

A: What would you do if you were offered an exciting job in London?
B: I would take the job because I love London.

Loans, credit lines and leasing

Speaking   **1**   Work in small groups. What is the difference between a loan, a credit line and a leasing agreement? Discuss.

Listening   **2**   ▶ 🎵 24   Listen to a banker talking to Mr Lizak, a new client. What type of business does Mr Lizak have?

3   ▶ 🎵 25   Now listen to the whole conversation and answer these questions.

1. Why does Mr Lizak need a new bank?
2. How is he planning to expand?
3. Which two products does the banker suggest for renting shops?
4. What solution does the banker suggest for buying the inventory?

Reading   **4**   Read the information about corporate products from a bank's intranet site and match 1–6 to a–f to make sentences.

1. Credit lines are useful ___
2. Liquidity means that a company has current assets ___
3. Property owned by a company can be used ___
4. The bank charges risky customers ___
5. If a customer wants to use a factory or a machine for a fixed period of time, ___
6. The amount an asset is worth at the end of the lease ___

a) to secure a loan.
b) is its residual value.
c) when a customer needs to have cash on hand.
d) a leasing agreement is usually the best way to do this.
e) they can change into cash.
f) higher interest rates.

CREDIT LINES

These are funds available to a borrower for a specific period, often as a flexible solution to cash flow problems. We look at each business case individually and work out the amount of the credit line with each customer. We look at the current assets because they can be changed into cash easily. This represents liquidity in the business. The customer pays interest on the amount borrowed and he or she can use more money than is in the account if they stay under the agreed limit. If the customers went over the limit for a period of time, there might be penalties. This type of financing is suitable for business opportunities, expansion plans and buying more inventory.

CORPORATE LOANS

Corporate loans can be arranged for up to ten years. These can be secured with real estate owned by the individual or the company. Again, we have to arrange these individually with customers. The customer receives the money immediately and the payments depend on the amount borrowed and the type of interest rate (fixed or variable) arranged, as well as the customer's creditworthiness. In general, when there is more risk, the bank sets a higher interest rate. There is a one-time loan origination fee and a penalty for early repayment. If a customer requested a corporate loan but didn't have enough security, we would conduct a full risk assessment.

LEASING AGREEMENTS

Leasing agreements are contracts giving the right to use an asset for a fixed period of time, in exchange for payments. The leasing agreement can be for a machine, piece of equipment or a building, which may also include the equipment or furnishings. The customer borrows the asset from us and pays for its use for a set period of time. At the end of the time the customer returns the asset to the bank or can buy it at its residual value. The residual value is how much it is worth at the end of the lease.

Language

Second conditional with modals

In second conditional sentences, we can use a modal verb instead of *would*. We often use *might*, *could* and *should*.	This **could** be fixed for five years **if** it **was** necessary. **If** the customers **went** over the limit for a period of time, there **might** be penalties. **If** a customer **requested** a corporate loan but didn't have enough security, you **should** conduct a full risk assessment.

5 Match 1–6 to a–f to make sentences.

1 If you wanted to own the property, ___
2 You should compare different bank products ___
3 We could offer you a fixed interest rate ___
4 We might look into issuing corporate bonds ___
5 If you had a problem with cash flow, ___
6 If you needed new machinery for your business, ___

a) if you took out a five-year loan.
b) you might think about a credit line for your business.
c) you could arrange to lease it.
d) if you wanted to choose the best one for your business.
e) you could buy it at the end of the leasing contract.
f) if you wanted to raise cash.

Speaking **6** Work in pairs. Discuss these questions about corporate products.

1 What should a customer do if he or she had problems with cash flow?
2 What might a customer do if he or she needed a new location for the business?
3 What products could a customer consider if he or she wanted to buy inventory or machinery?

If a customer had problems with cash flow, he or she should …

7 Work in pairs. Student A, look at the information on this page. Student B, look at the information on page 73. Follow the instructions.

Student A

1 You have been with a small local bank for many years. However, your business is expanding and you need to find a larger factory. You are talking to a new banker. Decide which goods or services you sell. Are you a manufacturer or a retailer? What is special about your business? Discuss corporate loans, credit lines or leasing agreements with the banker. Decide which one is best for you.

2 Swap roles. You are a banker. A new customer has come to you. Find out about his/her business and decide what he/she needs.

Writing **8** You are a banker. Write a letter to the customer in 7 with your recommendations. Remember to give reasons. Use the information in 4 and the audio script for track 25 on pages 78–79 to help you. Write 80–100 words.

> Dear Mr/Ms ...,
> I am writing to ...
>
>
> Yours sincerely,

Company restructuring and loan modification

Speaking **1** Work in pairs. What's happening in illustrations A–D? Why did it happen? What might happen next? How would you prevent this from happening if your company had a serious problem with debts?

Vocabulary **2** Complete these definitions of common word partnerships with the verbs in the box.

generate	liquidate	manage	modify	recover	refinance	restructure	settle

1 'To _____ bills with creditors' means to pay people or companies you owe money to.
2 'To _____ a loan' means to make changes to a loan agreement.
3 'To _____ a company' means to change business practices.
4 'To _____ a debt' means to be paid back when you don't expect to be.
5 'To _____ cash' means to raise funds.
6 'To _____ assets' means to sell property for cash.
7 'To _____ a loan' means to replace one loan with another at a lower rate of interest.
8 'To _____ debt' means to find a strategy to help an individual or company pay their bills.

3 Match 1–6 to a–f to make common word partnerships often used to talk about loan modification.

1 ☐ restructure   a) strategies
2 ☐ make   b) your costs
3 ☐ discuss   c) cash
4 ☐ generate   d) your debt
5 ☐ cut   e) a list of creditors
6 ☐ manage   f) the company

Listening **4** ▶ 🎧 26 Mr Kowalski, a businessman, has an appointment to talk to Karl Mayer in the Loan Modification Department. Listen to their conversation and number the phrases in 3 in the order you hear them.

5 Listen again and answer these questions.

1 What problem is Mr Kowalski having in his company?
2 What is the first step that Karl recommends?
3 What does Karl say about generating cash?
4 What does Karl suggest that Mr Kowalski do to pay off his creditors?
5 What is Karl's suggestion regarding the money the company owes the bank?
6 Why is the bank interested in helping Mr Kowalski with this problem?

Language

Making suggestions and recommendations

Why don't we *take a look at the figures?*
I would like to recommend *an external adviser to come and talk to you.*
We could *arrange a meeting within a few days.*
Would you be willing to consider *restructuring the company?*
I would suggest *liquidating assets.*
What about *selling off some buildings?*

6 Match 1–5 to a–e to make sentences for suggestions and recommendations.

1 Why don't we	a) to consider selling some of your property?
2 I would suggest	b) a way to generate cash.
3 What about	c) extending the line of credit.
4 I would like to recommend	d) look for alternative financing?
5 Would you be willing	e) restructuring the company?

Speaking **7** Work in pairs. What do you think loan modification strategy is? Why do you think it might be important for the bank? Discuss.

Reading **8** Read the letter Mr Mayer wrote to Mr Kowalski after their conversation and answer these questions.

1 What does 'default on a loan' mean?
2 What is a non-performing loan?
3 What does a turnaround professional do?
4 What are some ways to modify a loan?

Dear Mr Kowalski,

I have looked carefully at your income statement and your cash flow statement. I see that you are in danger of (1) <u>defaulting on your loan</u>. If you do not pay us back, we will have to reclassify the debt as a (2) <u>non-performing loan</u>.

We have decided to appoint a (3) <u>turnaround professional</u> to help you change the way your company works. By restructuring the company you should be able to generate some cash. You may need to liquidate some assets as we mentioned. You will have to think about which assets you can sell. It is also important that your company works more efficiently. The external adviser can help you to (4) <u>streamline some of your processes</u> and will speak with your creditors and help you to manage your debt.

After these steps have been taken, we can discuss changing your loan. We can make the period of time longer by (5) <u>extending the term</u>, for example. We may also think about charging interest only for a time. It is very important that we come to an agreement about the loan modification. Our goal is to help you (6) <u>stay in business</u>.

Please let me know if you have any questions.

Yours sincerely,

Karl Mayer

---

9 Read the letter in 8 again and match the underlined phrases 1–6 to a–f.

a) simplify the way things are done in a company ____
b) a debt in danger of not being paid back ____
c) have a longer time to pay back a debt ____
d) failure to pay back money ____
e) a person who helps with the reorganisation of a company ____
f) continue operations as a company ____

Bankruptcy

Speaking **1** Work in pairs. Discuss these questions.

1 What do you know about bankruptcy in your country? What are the different types?
2 Which companies have gone bankrupt in the last year? Do you see signs like the one in the photo? Why do you think this happens?

Reading **2** Fred Brown, a member of the board of Pools & Spas Ltd, has to explain a difficult situation to the managers in his company. Complete the explanation he is preparing for his colleagues with the words in the box.

> assets   bankruptcy   creditors   debts   loans   machinery   obligations   repayments

I am sorry to inform you that we have been unable to meet our (1) _____ to our suppliers and bank since the recession began. Two years ago we lost a lot of business but have hoped that the situation would improve. Unfortunately, we still have a lack of liquidity. Therefore, we have had to declare (2) _____ . This is a legal proceeding which allows our creditors to recover some of the money we owe them. The court consolidates our (3) _____ and decides how to pay our creditors. We also have to repay the money we borrowed and distribute some of our (4) _____ fairly. Now that the bankruptcy proceedings have begun, we no longer have to keep up our (5) _____ to the bank.

This is a voluntary bankruptcy; this means *we* have decided to do this. We did not want to wait for our creditors to start the bankruptcy proceedings. We hope that this will give us a fresh start once we have paid part of our debts to our (6) _____ .

I think if we waited, things would be much worse. Then our creditors may have wanted us to liquidate all of our assets to pay them. We did not want to auction off (7) _____ . We were also in danger of foreclosure; this means that the bank could take our buildings and sell them to raise cash to pay off our debts. This way we will be relieved of further liability and can try to reorganise the company. We hope to renegotiate some of the (8) _____ and pay back as much as possible.

Thank you all for your understanding at this difficult time.

Language

Past simple and present perfect

We use the **past simple** to talk about finished actions or situations in the past.	*Two years ago we **lost** a lot of business.*
We use the **present perfect** to talk about actions which have not finished or which happened in the past and have an effect on the present.	*Now that the bankruptcy proceedings **have begun**, we no longer have to keep up our repayments.*

3 Complete these sentences with the correct past simple or present perfect form of the verbs in brackets.

1 We _____ (have) problems since our largest client _____ (go) out of business.
2 We _____ (offer) this product for years and it is still very successful.
3 The recession _____ (cause) many problems at the beginning but we _____ (recover) and we are earning money again.
4 We _____ (start) the business ten years ago and _____ (expand) into new markets last year.

Review

Vocabulary **1** Match 1–8 to a–h to make sentences.

1	When companies cannot meet	a)	the money they lent.
2	They had to liquidate	b)	cash to pay their bills.
3	The adviser helped them manage	c)	bankruptcy and let the court handle the debts.
4	When a company defaults	d)	their obligations, they may have to go into bankruptcy proceedings.
5	The last step may be to declare	e)	a loan, it is better than not paying it at all.
6	If it is possible to modify	f)	their debt.
7	The creditors want to recover	g)	assets to pay their creditors.
8	They may need to generate	h)	on a loan, it can be expensive for the bank.

Language **2** Use these prompts to write second conditional sentences about corporate banking.

1 my credit line / extend / to €80,000 → I / could buy / more inventory
2 we / might try / to produce a new product line → we / get / the bank loan
3 they / default / on the loan → we / not get back / the capital we lent
4 we / declare / bankruptcy → we / not have to / pay
5 I / advise / you to modify your loan → you / have / cash flow problems

3 Complete these sentences using the correct present perfect, past simple or second conditional form of the verbs in brackets.

1 If I _____ (know) how to help them restructure the company, I would do it.
2 We _____ (have) this company as our client since 2010.
3 Last year the company _____ (declare) bankruptcy because they could not pay their creditors.
4 If we _____ (arrange) a loan, we _____ (can move) into a new shop.
5 Since the recession _____ (begin), we _____ (lose) many of our customers.

Speaking **4** Work in pairs. Complete these sentences.

1 We would liquidate assets if ....
2 We could expand the business if ...
3 The bank would lend us money if ...
4 If I had a great business idea, I would ...
5 If we had a cash flow problem, we could ...
6 I might need a letter of credit if ...

5 Work in pairs. When would you recommend these products and solutions to customers?

bankruptcy   credit line   leasing contract   letter of credit   loan modification
corporate loan

I would recommend ... if ...

6 Work in pairs. Student A, you are the customer. Student B, you are the banker. Student A, describe your problem to Student B. Student B, use the phrases for making suggestions and recommendations on page 57 to recommend two of the products in 5. Then swap roles and repeat the activity.

8

Central banks and banking regulations

- talk about central banks and their functions
- understand the business cycle and liquidity in the market
- talk about the economic trends
- describe graphs

National and central banks

Speaking **1** Work in pairs. Do this quiz. Then compare your answers with another pair.

1 Central banks are responsible for
  a) setting fees for current accounts.   b) keeping prices stable.
2 The European Central Bank (ECB) has to
  a) supply all the money for the euro-zone. b) produce financial data.
3 Many central banks
  a) keep reserves for other banks.   b) keep deposit accounts for governments.

Reading **2** Read these forum posts on central and national banks and check your answers in 1.

Bob, USA
Do we need the Federal Reserve in the USA? Why should we pay taxes to have another big bank?

Katia, German National Bank
Central or national banks help both the government and the other banks in the country. The basic function of a central or national bank is maintaining price stability by using a variety of methods. In many cases, the role of a central bank is encouraging financial stability. Sometimes a central bank has a monitoring role which may involve supervising the commercial banks. It often holds reserves for the other banks. In some countries the central bank controls the supply of money by deciding how much money other banks have to hold as reserves. In many countries the central bank issues and prints the currency. Some also manage the exchange rate of a country's currency.

Joëlle, France
What is the purpose of the European Central Bank?

Marie, consultant for the ECB, Belgium
The ECB is very important to the euro-zone. Its main function is keeping prices stable in the euro-zone and inflation just under two percent. The ECB is the central bank for the euro, the common currency in the European Union euro-zone member states. The first task of the ECB is deciding on and implementing monetary policy. This includes setting the interest rates for banks in the euro-zone. Then the banks decide how much interest to charge or pay customers for their business. It is also responsible for carrying out foreign exchange. Holding and managing the official foreign reserves of the euro area countries is a very important job for the ECB. In addition, the ECB has to regulate the payment systems within the euro-zone and make sure that it works without problems. Keeping the countries within the euro-zone economically stable is a very important function of the ECB.

Ania, Poland
Who makes the euro coins for each country? And what else does the ECB do? Can't the National Bank of Poland just do everything we need?

Franz, ECB, Germany
There are other jobs that the ECB does. One is deciding when to issue banknotes and coins within the euro area. The ECB is the only organisation which can authorise this. However, individual countries are responsible for minting their own coins. Another important task is collecting, analysing and publishing financial statistics. These are necessary for the ECB to decide on monetary policy and to carry out its other tasks.

---

3 Read the forum posts in 2 again. Which sentence is correct?

1 Keeping prices stable is an important function for central banks such as the ECB. Gathering statistical information helps them with monetary policy.
2 Keeping prices stable, printing banknotes and minting coins are responsibilities common to all central banks.

Vocabulary **4** Find words or phrases in the forum posts in 2 that match these definitions.

1 print money or mint coins (Katia) _____
2 money a bank needs to keep for possible future withdrawals (Katia) _____
3 making sure that costs for goods and services do not change much (Marie) _____
4 a general increase in the price of goods and services (Marie) _____
5 changing one currency for another (Marie) _____
6 making something public in writing (Franz) _____

Speaking **5** Work in small groups. Make notes from one of the posts in 2 and tell your group about it using your notes. Then discuss these questions.

1 Which responsibilities are common to all central banks and which only concern some central banks?
2 Talk about the central bank in your country and what it does.

Language

Gerund as subject and object	
A verb in the -ing form (**gerund**) can work as a noun and be the subject or the object of a sentence.	*Holding* the foreign reserves of the country is a task of many central banks.
We often use the gerund with the verb *be* but we can also use it with other verbs.	*Maintaining* price stability helps the economy. This includes **setting** the interest rates.

6 Complete the headings for this leaflet. Use the gerund of the verbs in the box.

authorise   guarantee   maintain   publish   set   supervise

Functions of central banks

(1) _____ financial information
One important duty of a central bank is to collect financial information and make it public.

(2) _____ commercial banks
Another responsibility of the central bank is often to oversee commercial banks.

(3) _____ new money
Central banks decide if new money needs to be printed.

(4) _____ liquidity
Another duty is to make sure that debts within the system can be paid.

(5) _____ interest rates
The central bank is responsible for deciding how high the interest rates should be.

(6) _____ price stability
One of the main duties of a central bank is keeping prices stable.

Speaking **7** Work in pairs. Talk about your job or a job you would like to have. Which of these activities is or would be the most or least challenging in that job? Put them in order and then explain your answer.

1 talking to clients
2 analysing financial information
3 having meetings
4 travelling
5 supervising junior colleagues
6 carrying out risk analysis
7 preparing financial documents
8 giving presentations

Liquidity and the business cycle

Speaking **1** Work in pairs. Discuss these questions.

1 How would you describe the economic situation in your country at the moment? Are people spending or saving money?
2 Do people and companies spend more or less money when loans are cheaper?
3 What do people tend to buy when there is more money in the market?

Reading **2** Read the text about liquidity and the business cycle and answer these questions.

1 What does liquidity mean?
2 What happens when banks have liquidity problems?
3 What do people do when they lose confidence in banks?
4 What do people spend money on when there is enough money in the system?
5 What do companies do when the economy is growing?
6 What is the meaning of inflation?
7 How does the central bank keep inflation low?
8 What happens when the economy contracts?

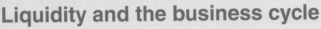

Liquidity and the business cycle

To understand the business cycle, we first have to understand liquidity. Liquidity tells us how easy it is to **sell an asset** for cash. In banks liquidity means **meeting obligations** without incurring losses. Therefore, **managing liquidity** is one of our most important tasks. When banks begin to have liquidity problems, they stop lending money. In addition, if all the depositors suddenly decide they want their money back, the entire market may be affected and we **lose consumer confidence**: people stop spending money.

The business cycle works like this: when the banks have been lending money and interest rates are low, there is growth in the economy. This is often a result of the central bank lowering interest rates. More people and companies **take out loans** and there is more money in the system. People **spend extra money** on non-essential goods like restaurants, free-time activities and holidays.

Once the economy begins to grow, other sectors begin to spend more money as well. Companies **invest in capital goods** such as machines, they buy more inventory and they ship more goods around the world. The economy is doing well but inflation starts. This means that goods and services get more expensive and the value of money goes down because people cannot buy as much as they could earlier.

This is the reason the central bank decides to **raise interest rates** again. Because the money banks borrow from the central bank is more expensive, they also raise their rates. In this case loans are not easy to get and people stop borrowing money.

The next stage in the cycle is called contraction. The economy has stopped growing and is beginning to shrink. But central banks see the problem and lower interest rates again. They hope this will motivate people to spend more money. Then the upward trend begins again.

Speaking **3** Work in small groups. Explain one of the stages of the business cycle to your group. Use the words in the box.

> assets inventory liquidity market motivate obligations ship goods
> shrink upward trend

4 Work in pairs. Choose five of the word partnerships in bold in the text in 2 and make definitions for them. Ask another pair to guess the correct word partnership for each definition.

5 Where in the business cycle is your country at the moment? What do you need to consider in order to decide this? Discuss.

Listening   **6**   ▶ 🔊 **27**   Listen to an investment manager talking to a journalist about the economy. Are these sentences *true* (T) or *false* (F)?

1   When consumers pay lower interest rates, their instalment payments go down. (T / F)
2   Lowering interest rates helps the economy very quickly. (T / F)
3   The currency of a country is always worth less when the central bank lowers interest rates. (T / F)
4   If governments invest in new projects, they will have more debts. (T / F)

7   Listen again and complete these slides from the interview.

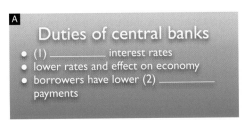

A
Duties of central banks
- (1) _____ interest rates
- lower rates and effect on economy
- borrowers have lower (2) _____ payments

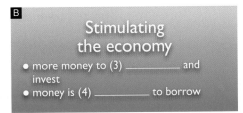

B
Stimulating the economy
- more money to (3) _____ and invest
- money is (4) _____ to borrow

C
Dangers of lower interest rates
- currency may lose (5) _____
- can (6) _____ to inflation

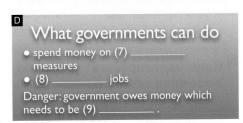

D
What governments can do
- spend money on (7) _____ measures
- (8) _____ jobs

Danger: government owes money which needs to be (9) _____ .

Language

Present perfect continuous

We use the **present perfect continuous** to talk about things that began in the past and continue into the present.	What **has been happening** in the economy?
We form the **present perfect continuous** with *have/has been* + *-ing*. We form negative sentences with *have/has not been* + *-ing* and questions with *have/has* + subject + *been* + *-ing*.	**Has** the economy **been growing**? No, the economy **hasn't been growing**. It **has been shrinking** since last year.
We use **for** when we talk about a period of time and **since** when we talk about a point in time.	Interest rates have been increasing **for** the last two quarters, **since** last July.

8   Complete these sentences with the correct present perfect continuous form of the verbs in brackets.

1   What topics _____ (you / discuss) in your training course?
2   I _____ (read) an interesting book on company finance.
3   The phone _____ (ring) all morning and I can't get any work done.
4   The customer _____ (not keep up) with his payments.

Speaking   **9**   Work in pairs. Discuss these questions.

1   What is the most interesting thing you have been doing for the last month?
2   What have the newspapers in your country been writing about?
3   Have people in your country been going out to restaurants and cinemas or taking holidays, or have they been saving money?

10   Work in small groups. Choose one of the slides in 7 and prepare a mini presentation for your group.

Regulations

Speaking **1** Work in pairs. Discuss these questions.

1 Do you know any regulations for banks in your country?
2 Why is it important to regulate the way banks do business? Do you think it is better for each country to regulate its banks or should there be worldwide laws?

FSA want public bank investigation *by Mary Almond*

The UK Financial Services Authority says the overseeing regulator should have power to investigate bank failures and publish such information.

Reading **2** Match these headlines from financial newspapers (1–6) to the article extracts (A–F).

1 Financial crisis makes governments take another look at risk

A The amount of core capital, which consists of retained profits plus shareholder equity, has been raised. Governments are making sure that banks keep enough money on hand for crisis situations.

2 Bank bankruptcies becoming problem for customers

B Banks often raise cash by finding more shareholders. Several banks are thinking about this and hoping that the public is interested. However, they do not want to reduce the dividend payments. The banks would like to keep their shareholders happy.

3 Are the risks worth the higher interest rates?

C When banks began failing due to liquidity problems, governments in many countries had to step in and help. Some banks had made very risky loans and could not recover the money. This meant that governments needed to think about new regulations for banks.

4 Core capital requirements set by governments

D Many banks were keeping a number of highly risky assets on their books. These loans were not backed up by collateral. However, the banks were able to charge much higher interest for them. The problems began when the borrowers began to default on these loans.

5 Ensuring bank liquidity

E When banks have a healthy balance of equity to risky assets, they can get through a crisis more easily. Banks need to keep enough core capital on hand if their risky investments do not work out.

6 Several banks issuing new shares

F People want to trust their banks. They need to know that their money is safe and they can withdraw it when they need it. Banks should be extremely careful with the money customers deposit. Losing customers' money through risky investments is certainly not what a trustworthy institution would do.

3 Find words in the extracts in 2 that match these definitions.

1 money the bank earned and kept (article A) _____
2 money paid to investors from the profits of a company (article B) _____
3 how quickly an asset can be converted to cash (article C) _____
4 not pay back money you owe (article D) _____
5 investments which are not guaranteed (article E) _____
6 something or someone you can believe in (article F) _____

Language

Defining relative clauses

A **defining relative clause** identifies which person or thing we are talking about. It gives essential, not just additional information. There is no comma between the main clause and the defining relative clause.

We can leave the relative pronoun out if it is the object of the relative clause but not if it is the subject.

	Subject of relative clause	Object of relative clause
People (*who, that*)	*People **who/that have been wanting to make investments** can now borrow money more cheaply.*	*The broker (**who/that**) **the firm employed** was very competent.*
Things (*which, that*)	*These are points **which/that are not finished from the last meeting**.*	*Reserves are the amount of cash (**which/ that**) **a bank needs to have**.*

4 Match 1–8 to a–h to make sentences, adding *who, which* or *that*. In which sentences can you leave out the relative pronoun?

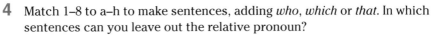

1 Regulations are rules
2 Auditors are staff members
3 We need a computer system
4 Money laundering is a system

5 A brokerage is a company
6 An insider trader is a person

7 An agenda is a document

8 The chair is the person

a) identifies credit card fraud.
b) sells stocks and bonds.
c) have to be followed.
d) everyone needs at the start of a meeting.
e) runs the meeting.
f) exchanges illegal money for legal money.
g) makes money illegally with inside knowledge about companies.
h) the bank employs to watch over other departments.

Speaking **5** Work in groups of four. You all work at Universal Bank. Look at this information and discuss the problem of liquidity facing the bank today.

1 Student A
You are in favour of highly risky assets.
➕ high interest rates, good earnings
➖ danger of defaults

2 Student B
You are in favour of keeping retained profits.
➕ high liquidity
➖ fewer investment possibilities

3 Student C
You are in favour of raising cash.
➕ Issuing shares brings new investors.
➖ Cutting back on dividends makes current investors unhappy.

4 Student D
You are in favour of making more lower risk investments.
➕ guarantee of repayment (or debt recovery)
➖ earn less money on interest

Writing **6** You work at Universal Bank. Write a short report to your boss on the problems facing the bank today. Write 80–100 words. Consider these points:

- capital requirements
- money laundering
- risk assessment when lending money
- credit card fraud

Introduction
I am writing this report to ...

Findings
I have discovered that ...

Conclusion and recommendations
In conclusion, I can say that ...

I recommend that we ...

Economic change

1 Read this extract from the annual report of Watford & Co. Does the graph illustrate interest rates or sales figures?

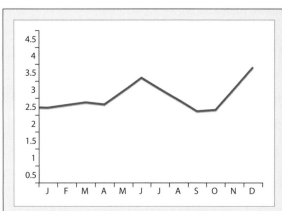

Over the last year we have seen different developments in both interest rates on our loans and our monthly sales figures. Interest rates began in January at 2.5%. They then <u>went up</u> slowly and <u>levelled off</u> in March at 2.65%. There was a modest <u>drop</u> back to 2.5% in April but in May we saw a noticeable <u>increase</u> until they <u>peaked</u> in June at 3.45%. In August they <u>fell</u> suddenly again and <u>bottomed out</u> at 2.3% in September. Then we saw a slight <u>rise</u> to 2.4% in October. Since then they have been <u>climbing</u> steadily and have now finished the year at 3.75%.

Our sales figures have also <u>fluctuated</u> in the past year. We started off in January with figures of €80,000 and this figure <u>grew</u> considerably over the next two months. They <u>reached</u> <u>a peak</u> in March at €120,000, fell slightly and then <u>remained stable</u> through April. Then in May we saw a modest <u>slump</u> to €100,000 but in June they <u>plunged</u> and continued to <u>decrease</u> rapidly until they <u>hit a low</u> at €45,000 in July and <u>stagnated</u> till the end of August. Luckily, they began to <u>recover</u> in September and <u>improved</u> consistently, reaching €75,000 in October. They then <u>soared</u> in November and we ended the year at €115,000 – a substantial improvement.

Vocabulary **2** Look at the underlined words in 1 and write them in the correct column. Mark the words as verbs (*v*), nouns (*n*) or verb phrases (*vp*).

Some verbs can also be used as nouns: *fall, drop, rise, increase, decrease, slump.*

Going up	Going down	Reaching the top	Reaching the bottom	Staying the same	Moving up and down

3 Match descriptions 1–4 to diagrams A–D.

1 Interest rates remained stable for a time and then fluctuated till they rose noticeably and peaked. ___
2 There was a substantial rise in profits, which then stagnated till they slumped and hit a low. ___
3 We saw a gradual increase in spending, which levelled off for a time, then climbed rapidly. ___
4 Sales figures soared, then went down moderately and then decreased rapidly. ___

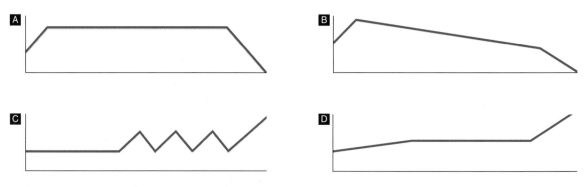

Speaking **4** Work in pairs. Student A, tell Student B about the sales figures in 1. Then swap roles. Student B, tell Student A about the interest rates in 1. Find different words to use than the ones in the text.

Review

1 Complete these sentences with the gerund of the verbs in the box.

authorise	control	invest	liquidate	maintain	meet	trade

1 One task of a central bank is _____ the issue of banknotes.
2 _____ consumer confidence is important for a healthy economy.
3 _____ obligations is necessary for banks who want to stay in business.
4 Companies _____ in capital goods is a sign that the economy is growing.
5 _____ stocks based on inside knowledge is illegal.
6 _____ inflation can be done by raising interest rates.
7 Raising capital can include _____ assets or finding new investors.

2 Complete these sentences with the correct present perfect continuous form of the verbs in brackets. Then join the sentences using *who* or *which*.

1 The head of the department _____ (speak) to employees. They are often late for work.
2 We _____ (implement) regulations for money laundering. They are designed to help us with the problem.
3 I _____ (write) emails to different people. They are all late with their loan repayments.
4 This is the report. Michael _____ (work on) it since Friday.
5 Since the financial crisis, governments _____ (create) new regulations. These regulations should help banks with liquidity problems.

Speaking **3** Work in small groups. Take turns to talk about the economy in your country. Use the phrases about trends on page 66.

4 Work in pairs. Student A, look at the information on this page. Student B, look at the information on page 73. Follow the instructions.

Student A
Describe this graph for Student B to draw. Use as many different trend words as you can. Then draw the graph Student B describes to you.

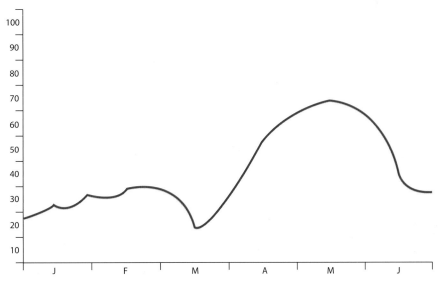

Writing **5** Write a paragraph describing the graph you drew in 4. Then compare your graph with the actual graph your partner described.

2 Products in retail banking

Bank products **Speaking exercise 8 page 13**

Student A

1   You are a banker. Use the phrases in the Language box on page 13 to find out what Student B, a customer, needs and to make suggestions.

2   Swap roles. You are the customer. You want to open an account to receive your salary. You also need to be able to withdraw money at weekends or in the evening. Answer Student B's questions.

4 Islamic banking

Review **Speaking exercise 5 page 35**

Student A

1   You work in the retail section of an Islamic bank. Your customer has some questions about buying a car. Use this information to tell him/her about the hire purchase agreement.

> **Ijarah Thumma Al Bai' (Hire purchase)**
>
> The bank buys an asset (such as a car) for a customer. The customer leases the asset from the bank. When this contract is over, the customer can buy the asset at a fixed price. The fixed price is higher because the customer pays the money back over a longer time.

2   Swap roles. You are a corporate customer at an Islamic bank and you have some questions about a joint venture. Ask your partner to explain this to you. Use questions like these:
   • How can I finance a business?
   • Is there an Islamic product for this?
   • Who contributes capital to it?
   • How do I earn money on the project?
   • How does the bank earn money?

5 The structure of a bank

The structure of the bank

Speaking exercise 7 page 39

Student A

Look at this organogram. Student B has the missing information. Ask questions to find the missing information and complete the organogram.

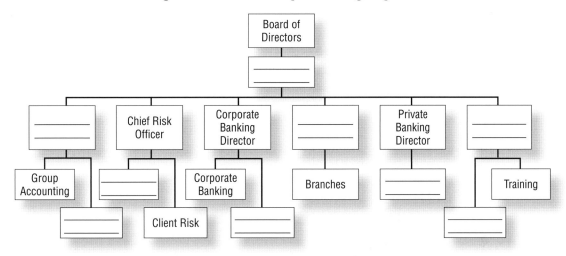

6 Finance in companies

The balance sheet

Speaking exercise 7 page 47

Student A

You have some of the assets of a company for one year and Student B has the liabilities. First find the missing words in equity/liabilities. Then read the information to each other and write down the figures. Look at your partner's information to check your answers.

This company has eleven million two hundred and thirteen thousand euros in assets.

The figures on the balance sheet are in thousands (000s):
€11,213 + 000 = €11,213,000

Balance sheet

Assets	€11,213	Equity	_____
Current assets	€5,145	Shareholders' equity	_____
			_____
Cash	€1,733	**Liabilities**	_____
Accounts receivable	€2,162		
Inventory	€1,250	*Current liabilities*	_____
Non-current assets	€6,068	Accounts payable	_____
Tangible assets	€4,046		_____
Intangible assets	€2,022	*Non-current liabilities*	_____
Total assets	**€11,213**	**Total liabilities + equity**	**€11,213**

Partner files: Student B

1 Money matters

Review **Speaking exercise 5 page 11**

Student B

You work for Homemaker Building Society. Answer a customer's questions.

Homemaker
and
Save and Build
are merging

Our building societies, **Homemaker** and *Save and Build*, are merging. We are closing some branches but we are also opening new, better ones. We are planning to offer more products with low interest rates ...

2 Products in retail banking

Bank products **Speaking exercise 8 page 13**

Student B

1   You are a customer. You have a current account. You want to be able to put money into a deposit account every month and to pay bills of differing amounts. Answer Student A's questions.

2   Swap roles. You are the banker. Use the phrases in the Language box on page 13 to find out what Student A, a customer, needs and to make suggestions.

Telephone helplines **Speaking exercise 3 page 16**

Student B

1   Listen to an online banking helpdesk representative and take notes.

2   Swap roles. You are an online banking helpdesk representative. Explain to a customer how to change a standing order using the information below.

1 log in – password	**4** type in amount
2 choose action – 'Standing order'	**5** click 'Enter'
3 click 'Change'	**6** print page

3 Personal loans and credit

Review **Speaking exercise 5 page 27**

Student B

1   You want to apply for a mortgage. Student A is the banker. Look at A and answer Student A's questions.

2   Swap roles. You work in banking. Student A wants to apply for a credit card. Look at B and ask questions to get the information you need to fill in the form.

A
- house – £250,000
- £50,000 deposit
- collateral: shares in a company
- 20-year mortgage
- fixed interest rate
- interest and capital payments

B
Customer's monthly salary: _____
Purpose: why customer needs card: _____
Additional functions: _____
Debit at end of month or carry balance? _____
Other features: _____

4 Islamic banking

Review **Speaking exercise 5 page 35**

Student B

1   You are a retail customer at an Islamic bank and you have some questions about buying a car. Ask your partner to explain this to you. Use questions like these:
- How can I buy a car without paying interest on the loan?
- Is there an Islamic product for this?
- Is it expensive?
- How does the bank earn money?

2   Swap roles. You work in the corporate banking section of an Islamic bank. Your customer has some questions about a joint venture. Use this information to tell him/her about the joint venture agreement.

> **Musharaka (Joint venture)**
>
> This is used for business partnerships. Each partner contributes capital to the project. The bank and the customer share the profits or the losses. This helps companies to finance projects. It is a type of PLS product.

5 The structure of a bank

The structure of the bank

Speaking exercise 7 page 39

Student B

Look at this organogram. Student A has the missing information. Ask questions to find the missing information and complete the organogram.

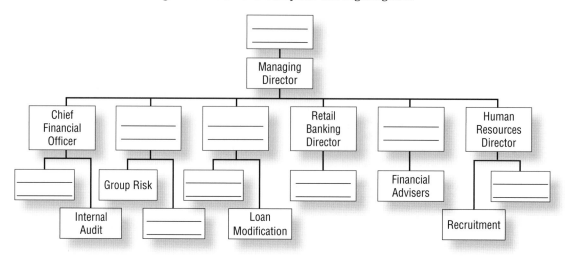

6 Finance in companies

The balance sheet

Speaking exercise 7 page 47

Student B

You have some of the liabilities of a company for one year and Student A has the assets. First find the missing words in assets. Then read the information to each other and write down the figures. Look at your partner's information to check your answers.

This company has two million and twelve hundred thousand in equity.

The figures on the balance sheet are in thousands (000s):
€11,213 + 000 = €11,213,000

Balance sheet

Assets	_____	Equity	€2,012
		Shareholders' equity	€1,300
Current assets	_____	Retained earnings	€712
Cash	_____	**Liabilities**	**€9,201**
Accounts receivable	_____		
_____	_____	*Current liabilities*	*€5,498*
Non-current assets	_____	Accounts payable	€3,678
		Taxes	€1,820
_____			
Intangible assets	_____	*Non-current liabilities*	*€3,703*
Total assets	**€11,213**	**Total liabilities + equity**	**€11,213**

7 Corporate banking

Loans, credit lines and leasing

Speaking exercise 7 page 55

Student B

1 You are a banker. A new customer has come to you. His/Her business is expanding and he/she needs to borrow money, or arrange a credit line or leasing agreement. Find out about your customer's business. Discuss the products and come to an agreement.

2 Swap roles. You are a businessperson. You have experienced cash flow problems and cannot pay your bank loan at the moment. You have some ideas of how you can restructure your company to save some money. You also want to liquidate some assets which you don't need for your production. Decide what type of business you have and list ways you plan to save money and generate cash. Try to convince your banker that you need some time to do this.

8 Central banks and banking regulations

Review

Speaking exercise 4 page 67

Student B

Draw the graph Student A describes. Then describe this graph for Student A to draw. Use as many different trend words as you can.

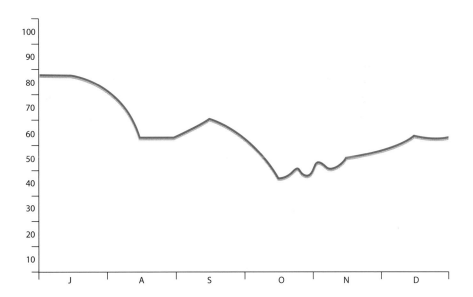

Audio script

Unit 1 Money matters

▶ 💿 02

1
A: Good morning. AFC Bank, can I help you?
B: Good morning. I am a customer of the bank and I want to borrow some money.
A: Yes, sir. Which department do you want? Er … what is the money for?
B: I want to buy a flat.
A: Just a moment. Oh yes, Mr Sharma is free.

2
A: Good morning, I am interested in shares of NewCom.
B: Oh yes. Just a moment. I see that the price is quite high at the moment.
A: I don't want to buy expensive shares and sell them for less. I don't want to make a loss.
B: I understand. AllTech looks good today. The demand for their shares is not so high at the moment.
A: That sounds interesting. I want to make a profit with this investment.

▶ 💿 03

1
A: What do you do every day?
B: I work with large companies. They call us when they want to buy another company, for example. Then they make a takeover bid.
A: And you help them?
B: Yes. They also sometimes want to join together with another company to make one company. That's a merger.

2
A: Is your job interesting?
B: Yes, it is. I help people when they buy a house or a flat.
A: Do you also offer current accounts and deposit accounts?
B: We offer some deposit accounts and we pay interest on them. But I don't usually open accounts. I mostly work with mortgages.

3
A: What happens in your job?
B: I do many different things. I sometimes open current accounts or deposit accounts.
A: Do you do other things, too?
B: Yes, I help people save for a pension. I usually work with private customers and small companies.

▶ 💿 04

1 My name is Katya. I work in a retail bank. I offer current accounts to customers. I also take deposits from customers and help them save for their pensions.
2 My name is Sylvester. I work in a building society. I also offer current accounts but I mostly arrange mortgages. I take deposits from customers and offer them special deposit accounts.

3 My name is Moira. I work in an investment bank. I arrange mergers and takeover bids for companies. I also give companies financial advice and help them sell their shares.

▶ 💿 05

1 We need a financial plan for the future. Do you have any ideas?
2 I want to buy a house. How much is the interest on a housing loan?
3 I need a place for important things. Do you have a place here at the bank?
4 We need some capital. Is it possible to sell shares of our company?
5 I want to save some money and get interest on it. What kind of account is good for me?
6 I need money for everyday things. What accounts do you offer?
7 Our company wants to buy another company. Can you help me with this?

Unit 2 Products in retail banking

▶ 💿 06

A: Good morning. Can I help you?
B: Yes, I need an account.
A: What kind of account do you need?
B: Next week I start my first job. I'm also moving to my first flat. I need an account so I can receive my salary and pay my bills.
A: We can open a current account for you. Then you can receive your salary by direct deposit.
B: What does that mean?
A: That means that your salary comes directly into your account every month. You do not need to deposit money yourself.
B: OK. I understand. And bills?
A: We can set up standing orders for you.
B: What are those?
A: With a standing order you can say how much you want to pay someone every month.
B: And when the bills are for different amounts? What can I do then?
A: Then I suggest we arrange direct debits. The person who gets the money from you sends us a bill and we pay it.
B: That sounds fine. What do I do when I need money?
A: You will get a bank card and then you will be able to use the cash dispenser to make withdrawals.
B: OK. Can we open the account today?
A: Of course. Just a moment and I'll just …

▶ 💿 07

A: Good afternoon. UBE Bank helpline. Can I help you?
B: Yes, I hope so. I am having problems with online banking.

A: What is the problem?
B: I have a password but it doesn't work.
A: OK. First I need your name.
B: Yes, it is Anish Chatterjee. That's A-N-I-S-H C-H-A-T-T-E-R-J-E-E.
A: Your password has five letters and two numbers.
B: Yes, that is right.
A: OK. First go to 'Log in' and put in your password.
B: OK, I'll do that now. And then?
A: After that click on 'Proceed' and you will see the page for your account.
B: Ah, I click on 'Proceed'. Yes, here is the page ...
A: Next, do you see the information on the right? It asks you what you want to do.
B: Yes, I see it. I want to look at my statement.
A: Then click on the button for 'Statement'. Do you see it now?
B: Yes, I do.
A: Good. Is there anything else?
B: No, I think I am all right now. And at the end I log out – is that right?
A: Yes. That's it.
B: Thank you so much.
A: No problem. Call anytime you need help. That's why we're here. Goodbye.
B: Goodbye.

Unit 3 Personal loans and credit

▶ 🎵 08

Do you travel the world? Does shopping everywhere sound interesting to you? Then call us to find out about our new multi-function Champion Credit Card! If you have a Champion card, you can pay for food, a hotel room, a concert ticket or rent a car without cash. If you choose the debit option, you can pay for your purchases immediately. When you have a Champion card, you can use ATMs everywhere – just arrange a credit limit with your bank. You can also carry a balance over from one month to the next. When you choose this option, your monthly statement shows you how much interest you have to pay. We know that young people like to travel, so you even get travel insurance with this card! You can also choose your repayment terms and get a PIN code for online shopping. If you lose your card, just call our helpline number. Contact us at any time if you have questions about the card. We will be happy to help you. What are you waiting for?

▶ 🎵 09

1 A: I think a pre-paid card is very good to have.
  B: I couldn't agree more but a multi-function card may be better.
  A: Why?
  B: If you have a multi-function card, you can use it like a credit card or withdraw money from an ATM. Then you only need one card.
  A: That's not a bad idea. I'll talk to my bank about one.

2 A: Do you need a credit card?
  B: No, I usually use cash. I don't want to borrow money and pay it back later.
  A: I see your point.
  B: Do you have one?

A: Yes, because I travel a lot. Don't you think they are useful in another country?
B: Yes, but I don't want to pay interest, so I just go to an ATM. Don't you think that is a good idea?
A: It is out of the question for me because sometimes I can't find an ATM and I always have my card with me. It's just easier.

▶ 🎵 10

[C = Caroline; M = Manager]
C: Do you have a minute? I need to talk to you about an account.
M: Yes, of course. What do you want to know?
C: Mr Müller often overdraws his account. This happens about every two months, when his expenses are higher than his income.
M: Yes, I see. Does he cover his overdraft regularly?
C: Yes, he does. He always deposits enough money to be in the black again.
M: Is the overdraft authorised? Does he also have to pay penalties when he overdraws his account?
C: He has an overdraft facility of 2,500 euros a month, so he doesn't have to pay bank charges. But he must pay interest when he is over that amount.
M: Does he know that he mustn't go over the limit?
C: Yes, he does, but his expenses are high. And then he has to pay interest on the overdraft. When his overdraft lasts for several weeks, it is expensive for him.
M: Yes, that's true. We charge more on overdrafts than on loans.
C: So isn't it better for him to apply for a personal loan?
M: Yes, I think so. It seems he has a cash flow problem. Do you want to talk to him about this?
C: OK. I can give him an application form and send him to a loan officer to talk about the terms and the instalments. We can suggest an appointment on Friday.

▶ 🎵 11

[C = Caroline; M = Mr Müller]
C: Good morning, Mr Müller. I need to talk to you about your account.
M: Is there a problem?
C: Not really. I just see that you often overdraw it and then have to pay interest on the overdraft amount.
M: Yes. I have my own company and we sometimes have cash flow problems.
C: I see.
M: If I do a job for a customer, I sometimes have to wait for several months for the money.
C: So you can't pay all your bills right away?
M: Right. That's why I must have an overdraft facility. It covers my expenses.
C: But it can be the most expensive way for you to borrow money.
M: Do you have a better idea?
C: If you have a short-term loan, you don't have to pay such high interest. The rates are lower than the overdraft facility.
M: Really? That sounds interesting.
C: I have an application form here.
M: What do I have to do?

C: You just need to fill it out and talk to a loan officer.

M: Do I need to do anything else?

C: No, you don't need to do anything else. You just have to give the loan officer information about your income and expenses. If you decide that a loan is a good idea, he will also explain the instalments to you.

M: Thank you very much.

C: No problem, Mr Müller.

Unit 4 Islamic banking

▶ 🔵 12

Good afternoon, everyone. How much did you know about Islamic banking before the seminar this morning? Now you are going to hear about our new section for Islamic banking. The idea for interest-free banking began during the time of the prophet Muhammad. People weren't allowed to charge or receive interest. However, for years customers weren't able to find Islamic banks. Many customers asked us about interest-free banking and other products. So we decided to open a section for these customers. First we needed a Shari'ah board because the banking laws had to follow Islamic economic policies. This board explained to us how everything worked. Finally, we offered our first interest-free accounts to customers. We have many other products as well and you will hear about them in tomorrow's seminar.

▶ 🔵 13

[PF = Peter Farrel; AF = Abdul Farak]

PF: Good afternoon, Mr Farak. Welcome to First Bank. Tell me, where did you use to have your accounts?

AF: Before this section of the bank opened, I used to go to a non-Islamic bank. I had a current account and a deposit account with AFG Bank. I used to get interest on both accounts. If I overdrew my current account, I paid interest on it. The interest on my savings account depended on the interest rates at the time.

PF: And did you use to borrow money from your bank?

AF: Oh yes, I used to borrow money. For example, I needed a loan to buy a car and I used to pay the bank the interest and the capital every month. I thought about a mortgage but I didn't want to pay interest for such a long time. Then you opened this section for Islamic banking. I closed my accounts and came here. I now have a current account and I like the idea that the bank keeps my money safe for me.

PF: And what about your overdraft? Was it very expensive?

AF: Yes, it was. Now, if I overdraw my current account, I pay a fee but no interest. I also have a fixed-term deposit account and earn money if the bank makes a profit. I don't get interest on either of the accounts.

PF: And what did you decide about your mortgage? Do you have one with us now?

AF: I have a special type of mortgage which follows Islamic law. I gave the bank a deposit and the bank bought my house. Now they rent it to me, so I don't have to pay interest. I pay the bank every month and soon I will own it completely. I am very happy that I found this bank and can get these products today.

PF: This is exactly why we opened this section. Many customers asked us about these products. We are very glad that you are one of our first customers in this new section of our bank.

▶ 🔵 14

1   I was thinking about starting a new business and I was looking for someone to help me. So I went to my bank. We talked about financing and they asked me lots of questions about my business plan. I think they're interested. They think I'll be able to make a profit with my ideas.

2   I need to buy some things for my business. They cost a lot of money. I was looking for different ways to pay for them, when I heard about a product at my bank. I talked to my banker and we discussed the things I need and how I can pay the bank back.

3   I have some money which I want to invest in a business. I was trying to find a partner, and was talking to a friend about the idea. He told me about this product at the bank. So yesterday I talked to my banker and we now have an agreement.

Unit 5 The structure of a bank

▶ 🔵 15

1   I take care of tailor-made products for corporate clients. I work in the Corporate Banking Department.

2   I am responsible for auditing the books of the bank. I have to make sure that everything we do is correct. I work in the Internal Audit Department.

3   I help my boss with the preparation of financial documents for the bank. I work in the Group Accounting Department.

4   We are in charge of modifying corporate loans when customers have cash flow problems. We help them to pay their loans back. I work in the Loan Modification Department.

5   We deal with managing investment portfolios for wealthy customers. I work in the Private Banking Department.

6   My department is in charge of recruiting new staff members. We also train existing staff to help them do their jobs better. I work in the Human Resources Department.

▶ 🔵 16

[A = Ali; J = Jo; D = Dan; S = Sarah]

A: My name is Ali. I really like my job in the bank. I report to my branch manager, who is above me in the hierarchy. I work with customers and sell standard products. I mostly work at the counter but sometimes I have to work at the computer or have meetings with customers to discuss things.

J: I am Jo. I am responsible for deciding if corporate customers get loans or not. I have to look at the company's finances and all their documents. Then I try to assess the risk. I have to make sure the company has a good credit rating and I expect them to pay the money back on time. When we have a problem, I talk to colleagues on the same level as me in the Loan Modification Department.

D: My name is Dan. I work for the HR director. I have an assistant who is below me. Together we are responsible for finding out what the other employees in the bank need. Then we decide which training sessions to offer and we set up different courses. We deal more with people than with money in our job.

S: I am Sarah. In my department we have to oversee the other departments. We are in charge of compliance. We make sure that everyone follows all the rules in the bank. We look at the books and how departments do things and we report to the Chief Financial Officer, who supervises our work. We are on the same level as our colleagues in the Group Accounting Department but we don't work together very often.

▶ 🔊 17

Good morning everyone and welcome to my presentation. My presentation is in three parts. First, I am going to tell you about how banks get money. Then you are going to hear some information about loans and credit lines. The last part of my presentation is going to be about interest rates and our profit margin. Please feel free to ask questions.

So to start off, how do banks get money? Customers open deposit accounts and give us money to keep safe for them. Sometimes they leave the money in the bank for many years. We use that money to make investments and loans.

Now moving on to loans and credit lines. Customers can borrow money from us in different ways. They can have an overdraft facility and borrow money for a short time. We earn money with these because we charge the customer interest. We also have credit lines for companies. This means they can borrow money up to a fixed amount and pay interest on it. These are for much higher amounts than overdraft facilities.

Finally, I am going to tell you about short- and long-term loans and interest rates. These have fixed monthly payments and the interest is included. With these loans we have a good idea of how much interest we earn. However, we also offer fixed and variable rates. These change when the interest rates change.

In conclusion, how do we make money? Our profit margin is the difference between the amount we charge for interest and the amount of interest we pay our customers. The most difficult part for us is to balance the short-term financial needs of customers with our long-term loans.

To sum up, you heard today about the money we 'borrow' from customers and the money we lend them. You also heard about different forms of borrowing, interest rates and our profit margin. Thank you very much for your attention. So, are there any questions?

Unit 6 Finance in companies

▶ 🔊 18

[I = Interviewer; SJ = Steve Jones]

I: Good morning, listeners. I'm here with Steve Jones of Events & Co. Steve, can you tell us about a recent event?

SJ: No problem – we've just finished one! The customer asked us to set up an evening to promote a new type of garden furniture. The event was in June, so we began to organise it in January. The cost for the event was €25,000 and we got €12,500 in January. We started to make a video for them and this cost us €2,800 altogether. Next we set up a photo shoot for advertising.

I: And how did that go?

SJ: Well, we planned this for the second week in February but had bad weather. We had to wait till the next week. So we had to pay the people who were in the shoot extra for their time. That cost us €2,700.

I: Oh! What did you have to do next?

SJ: The next step was to find someone to be in charge of the evening. We found someone for €2,200. But he got another job and we had to look again in March. In the end, we paid €3,500 for the new person we found.

I: Mm, was that the end of the problems?

SJ: Not completely. We had a contract with the location and the deposit was €2,500 in April. We didn't have enough cash then and used our overdraft. This cost us €150 in interest.

I: Sounds complicated to me. And then what happened?

SJ: In May another client suddenly cancelled an order. Then we had to arrange a short-term loan with the bank for €15,000. The first thing we did was pay €3,000 for the food.

I: Mhm. And then what happened?

SJ: We hoped our problems were over. But at the beginning of June the company told us that only half of their guests were coming, so we had to change the order for the food. We missed the cancellation deadline, so our costs came to an extra €1,500.

I: Oh! And how did the event go?

SJ: The event was a big success and we made money on it. In June we invoiced the company for the rest of the money they owed us. In July they paid us the rest, so we got €12,500. Then we were able to pay back the bank loan of €15,000 plus the interest, which came to €375.

▶ 🔊 19

1	548,209,120
2	43,890,200
3	97,009,776,231
4	867,334,097,124
5	89,450,342
6	39,548

▶ 🔊 20

Trainee: So what's an income statement exactly?

Trainer: Well, an income statement shows the operating revenues and expenses of a company for one year. It is used with the balance sheet to find out about the financial position of a company. You see these numbers written in brackets here? They are minus numbers.

▶ 🔊 21

So, let's take a look at this income statement and the one from last year. You can see that the company has a net profit after tax of €1,046 million. This figure is a result of the sales minus the operating expenses, interest and taxes. But we should look at the net profit margin because it is important for this to be over ten percent. To find it, we divide the net profit after tax by the sales. This means that we divide the €1,046 million by €8,900 million. This gives us a percentage of 11.75 percent. That is a good sign because it is over ten percent. Let's go to last year's income statement. Here we see that the company had 7.6 million in sales. This was lower than this year. However, their net profit after tax was €996,000, meaning that the net profit margin last year was higher, at 13 percent. The lower profit margin this year might mean that their performance is not as good as it was last year. However, it could also mean that they had other expenses. So we have to look at other parts of the income statement to decide if they are doing better or not.

Another thing we need to see is how other companies in the same field are doing. It could also mean that the whole sector had problems last year. So it is necessary to compare these figures with other companies. In addition, we will need to check the balance sheet and their other financial documents before we make a final decision. Do you have any questions?

Unit 7 Corporate banking

▶ 🎧 22

[M = Marta; P = Piotr]
M: Can you tell me what happens here in this department? How is it different from the Retail Banking Department?
P: I think the main difference is that we offer tailor-made products to most of our clients. We offer standard products such as current accounts as well but usually we need to find out more exactly what the client needs. We also deal with much larger amounts of money.
M: And what types of jobs are there in this department?
P: Well, I began as a credit analyst. That means I had to look carefully at the balance sheets and other financial documents and business plans. Then I had to carry out a risk assessment.
M: What is that?
P: A risk assessment finds out if a customer is creditworthy. Basically, I had to ask myself, 'Could a client pay us back if we lent him or her money?'. I had to look at lots of different documents to get this answer. Last year, however, I became a relationship manager and began to work directly with clients.
M: So your job is different now?
P: Yes, now I help corporate clients with lots of different matters. This can be financing new projects, helping them with expansion or arranging special loans, for example.

▶ 🎧 23

1 A: Good morning, Ms Wichinski. I have a question for you. If I wanted to buy goods from Indonesia and import them to Poland, what would I need to do?
   B: Do you have the information about the seller with you, Mr Kosnik?

A: Yes, here it is. Ameyah Batak. The company is in Jakarta. Here is the full address and the details of the goods I plan to import.
B: Very good. It looks like you need a letter of credit. I will start work on this right away.
A: Thank you very much.

2 A: Good afternoon, Mr Ferrando. I have asked you to come and talk to me because I have some questions about your cash flow statement and the loan application you made with us.
   B: Is there a problem?
   A: Well, we are looking carefully at your revenues and expenses because we are worried about your ability to pay debts. In addition, the amount of money you owe seems to be quite high.
   B: Yes, but if you look at our income statement, you will see that our net profit margin is higher this year than last year.
   A: I see. If you gave us your income statements for the past several years, we would have a better idea of your company's situation. I am sure we will come to an agreement once we have all the facts.

3 A: Ms Park. How can I help you today?
   B: I wanted to speak to you about our business plans. A business adviser told me that if we had the chance to buy several new shops, we should do this. What do you think?
   A: Well, you have been very successful in the last year, so I think it would be a good idea.
   B: And if I needed a credit line or a loan, would you be able to help me?
   A: Of course. I know your company well and I am sure we can find the best solution for you. Why don't we take a look at the figures?

▶ 🎧 24

[PK = Piotr Kot; L = Mr Lizak]
PK: Good afternoon, Mr Lizak. What can I do for you?
L: Hello, Mr Kot. I'm interested in bringing my business to your bank.
PK: May I ask why you are looking for a new bank?
L: Of course. I started my textile business six years ago and stayed with my small local bank. But my business has grown and I now have the chance to expand into several new cities. Therefore, I need financing, and my bank cannot handle these needs.
PK: I see. What kind of expansion are you planning?
L: I buy clothing and accessories from several different suppliers. As my business is going well, I need to expand. I plan to rent several shops but need to buy furnishings such as shelves and display areas.

▶ 🎧 25

[PK = Piotr Kot; L = Mr Lizak]
PK: Good afternoon, Mr Lizak. What can I do for you?
L: Hello, Mr Kot. I'm interested in bringing my business to your bank.
PK: May I ask why you are looking for a new bank?
L: Of course. I started my textile business six years ago and stayed with my small local bank. But my business has grown and I now have the chance to expand into several new cities. Therefore, I need financing and my bank cannot handle these needs.

PK: I see. What kind of expansion are you planning?

L: I buy clothing and accessories from several different suppliers. As my business is going well, I need to expand. I plan to rent several shops but need to buy furnishings such as shelves and display areas.

PK: Do you also need to buy more inventory?

L: Yes, that as well. The problem is that I don't know exactly how much I will sell but I have to pay my suppliers within a short time.

PK: So, it sounds like you need two or three different products. The first one I would suggest is a leasing agreement. If you found shops with the necessary furnishings, we could arrange the leasing contract for you. Then you would have monthly payments for as long as the lease, and you could decide at the end if you want to continue it or not.

L: What would the other possibility be?

PK: Well, we could also look into a corporate loan. This could be fixed for five years if it was necessary, for example. Then you could buy all your furnishings and other things you needed and pay the instalments monthly or quarterly.

L: Is there anything else I would need?

PK: We should think about a credit line if you wanted to buy inventory for the new shops.

L: And how would that work?

PK: You could overdraw your account up to a certain limit and pay only interest but no penalties. If your liquidity was a problem, you might think about this option. And if you didn't need to overdraw your account, you wouldn't pay anything. If you didn't have a credit line, it would be expensive if you overdrew your account.

L: You have given me a great deal to think about! I will take a look at all these possibilities and come and talk to you again next week.

▶ 🎧 26

[KM = Karl Mayer; K = Mr Kowalski]

KM: Good afternoon, Mr Kowalski. I'm afraid we have to discuss the problems you are having with profit and liquidity in your company.

K: Yes, I know. We're having a real problem paying our bills at the moment, Mr Mayer.

KM: I think we first need to look into a way to manage your debt. I would like to recommend an outside adviser to come and talk to you. We have worked with several firms that do this type of work.

K: What would happen if we agreed to see an outside adviser?

KM: We could arrange a meeting within a few days. The adviser would visit you on your premises.

K: Do you think if we can get some advice on how to generate cash, we could solve the problem?

KM: I think we need to do more than that. Would you be willing to consider restructuring the company if necessary?

K: Yes, I would.

KM: The adviser will then work with you to look at ways to cut your costs and create profit. This may involve changing suppliers or your accounting system, or even reducing the number of staff you have.

K: OK. And the next step?

KM: Well, we will need to discuss the strategies the adviser recommends. The first thing you need to do is make a list of all the creditors you have and how much you owe them.

K: OK, I can put that together for you.

KM: Then I would suggest liquidating some assets to pay them off.

K: What about selling off some buildings we don't need for production at the moment?

KM: That could be a possibility. This is the type of advice our restructuring expert can give you. But settling bills with creditors is the first step.

K: And then?

KM: Once we have done that, we will see where we are. The next step will be to discuss how we can modify your loan with us. We will need to look into changing the terms and the repayments.

K: Thank you so much. I appreciate this help.

KM: This is what I am here for. It's also in our interest to help you as we would like to recover our money, too. I think if we work together on this problem, we will find a solution for both of us.

Unit 8 Central banks and banking regulations

▶ 🎧 27

[J = Julia; R = Robert]

J: Good morning. Welcome to our TV news show about the economy. I am here with Robert Jones, who is going to tell us about ways to help the economy grow.

R: Good morning, Julia. Nice to be here. Well, there are different ways to help the economy when it has been having growth problems. You know one of the duties of a central bank is to regulate interest rates, for example by lowering them. Borrowers who have been paying high interest rates suddenly have lower instalment payments.

J: How does this help?

R: This can stimulate the economy because these people have more money to spend. Others who have been wanting to make investments can now borrow money more cheaply.

J: Does it happen immediately?

R: After the central bank has lowered the interest rates, it takes about two or three quarters until this helps the economy. One problem is that the currency of a country may also lose value. In addition, growth stimulated by more money in the system can lead to inflation.

J: And what can governments do?

R: The government can spend money on stimulus measures like building schools and highways, or putting money into the public transport system. This creates jobs, and when people are working, the economy can begin to grow again. The problem here is that the government will then owe money which has to be repaid.

J: Anything else?

R: Another way relies on laws and regulations by the government such as lowering taxes and so on ...

Pearson Education Limited

Edinburgh Gate

Harlow

Essex CM20 2JE

England

and Associated Companies throughout the world.

www.pearsonelt.com

First published 2012

ISBN: 978-1-4082-6989-3

Set in ITC Cheltenham Book

Printed by Graficas Estella, Spain

Acknowledgements

The publishers and author would like to thank the following people for their feedback and comments during the development of the material:

Melissa Bodola, USA; Chris Darkens, Senior Manager, Bank of England, UK; Gottfried Fuchs and Robert Rieder, Steiermärkische Sparkasse, Austria; Matthew Harris, BSc, Associate Chartered Accountant, UK; Alma Lojo, Austria; Chris Roland, Spain; Bernice Rosenberg, USA; Stefan Roth, CEO, Eventkartell, Austria; Brenda M. Sorg, VP, Wells Fargo Private Bank, USA; Ian Stride, Spain

The publisher would like to thank the following for their kind permission to reproduce their photographs:

(Key: b-bottom; c-centre; l-left; r-right; t-top)

4 Fotolia.com: Andrey Andreev #4590405. **5 Shutterstock.com:** Goodluz. **7 Fotolia.com:** auremar #33404285. **8 Alamy Images:** Clive Sawyer (A). **Rex Features:** Sipa Press (C); Ray Tang (B). **10 Alamy Images:** Peter Cavanagh. **15 Shutterstock.com:** StockLite. **16 Fotolia.com:** Yuri Arcurs#20567436. **18 Shutterstock. com:** Supri Suharjoto. **20 Alamy Images:** Jim Wileman. **23 Rex Features:** John Powell. **24 Pearson Education Ltd:** Photodisc / Brofsky Studio Inc.. **26 Shutterstock.com:** rosesmith. **29 Alamy Images:** Kevpix. **32 Shutterstock. com:** slava296. **33 Fotolia.com:** poco_bw #15746654 (l). **Shutterstock.com:** Zurijeta (c); picturepartners (r). **36 Fotolia.com:** aliola #10171903. **37 Getty Images:** Stephan Hoeck. **42 SuperStock:** View Pictures Ltd. **44 Alamy Images:** moodboard. **46 Fotolia.com:** Pavel Losevsky #5123228. **49 Shutterstock.com:** ArtyFree. **52 Getty Images:** Paul Bowen. **53 Fotolia.com:** Margo Harrison #8814083. **54 Shutterstock.com:** Rido. **58 Shutterstock. com:** Simon Smith. **60 Getty Images:** Jens Kuhfs. **62 Shutterstock.com:** Palych1378. **65 Fotolia.com:** Yuri Arcurs #20569250.

Cover images: *Front:* **Getty Images:** travelstock44 background, Walter Bibikow / age fotostock l; **Shutterstock.com:** Rido c; **SuperStock:** James Steidl / SuperFusion r

All other images © Pearson Education

Every effort has been made to trace the copyright holders and we apologise in advance for any unintentional omissions. We would be pleased to insert the appropriate acknowledgement in any subsequent edition of this publication.